Aggressive
Good Faith
and
Successful
Claims Handling

Aggressive
Good Faith
and
Successful
Claims Handling

WILLIS PARK ROKES, J.D., Ph.D.
Peter Kiewit Distinguished Professor
Law and Insurance
University of Nebraska at Omaha

First Edition • 1987

INSURANCE INSTITUTE OF AMERICA
720 Providence Road, Malvern, Pennsylvania 19355-0770

Foreword

Over the years, the American Institute for Property and Liability Underwriters and the Insurance Institute of America have responded to the educational needs of the property and liability insurance industry by developing courses and administering national examinations specifically for insurance personnel. These companion nonprofit educational organizations receive the support of the insurance industry in fulfilling this need.

The American Institute maintains and administers the program leading to the Chartered Property Casualty Underwriter (CPCU) professional designation.

The Insurance Institute of America offers a wide range of associate designation and certificate programs in the following technical and managerial disciplines:

Accredited Adviser in Insurance (AAI)
Associate in Claims (AIC)
Associate in Underwriting (AU)
Associate in Risk Management (ARM)
Associate in Loss Control Management (ALCM)
Associate in Premium Auditing (APA)
Associate in Management (AIM)
Associate in Research and Planning (ARP)
Associate in Insurance Accounting and Finance (AIAF)
Associate in Automation Management (AAM)
Associate in Marine Insurance Management (AMIM)
Certificate in General Insurance
Certificate in Supervisory Management
Certificate in Introduction to Property and Liability Insurance

The Associate in Claims (AIC) designation program was first

offered in 1963. It was originally co-sponsored by the National Association of Independent Insurance Adjusters and has been widely used by members of that association and many insurance companies to help meet the educational needs of their claim personnel. This text was developed as part of a general reorganization of the program's curriculum. It is the second Institute-published text to be assigned in the AIC program.

As with all Institute publications, this text has been extensively reviewed by a group of academic and industry experts, and they are recognized in the authors' preface. Throughout the development of this series of texts, it has been—and will continue to be—necessary to draw on the knowledge and skills of Institute personnel. These individuals will receive no royalties on texts sold; their writing responsibilities are seen as an integral part of their professional duties. We have proceeded in this way to avoid any possibility of conflict of interests.

We invite and welcome any and all criticisms of our publications. It is only with such comments that we can hope to provide high quality study materials. Comments should be directed to the Curriculum Department of the Institutes.

Norman A. Baglini, Ph.D., CPCU, CLU, AU
President

Preface

Aggressive Good Faith and Successful Claims Handling is the second prescribed reading for the AIC 33 course, the first of the four courses comprising the Associate in Claims program of the Insurance Institute of America. The text, together with *Human Relations In Handling Insurance Claims*, represents a cornerstone of the foundation course devoted to the all-important relationship between the claims person and the public. While *Human Relations* is designed to impart the knowledge and skills necessary for one-on-one contacts in claims work, the present work teaches adjusters to cope successfully with rules and laws formulated to protect the public good in insurance claims relationships. By its nature it is equally an essential text and reference for claims practitioners in the property and liability areas, indeed in all types of claims work.

The first chapter lays the groundwork for an understanding of today's claims practices by a brief glance at claims handling relations of the fifties and early sixties and the gradual socio-legal changes that lead to today's claims environment. Chapter 2 is devoted to the concept of "bad faith" and specifically to the development of modern bad faith law and commonly encountered bad faith cases. Chapter 3 deals with the concept of punitive damages, its elements, and its relationship to both claims handling and to insurance coverage. Chapter 4 discusses the most significant statutory regulation of insurance claims practices. The "Unfair Claims Settlement Practices" acts define the everyday reality in almost all jurisdictions for adjusters and claims representatives. The chapter examines the typical act in detail and explains its significance to claims personnel. The text concludes with concrete guidelines for a claims handling attitude focused on positive good faith practices that is not only mandated by law but is also designed to bring desirable results.

We want to express our gratitude to Charles Barr, Esquire, CPCU, and John N. Lemieux, Esquire, CPCU, who reviewed the manuscript.

Their prompt and conscientious work has greatly contributed to insuring both technical accuracy and stylistic quality.

Willis Park Rokes

Table of Contents

CHAPTER 1

Then and Now

INTRODUCTION

Things have changed in the insurance claims handling profession. As a new insurance claims adjuster, you are operating in an entirely new social and legal atmosphere from that which existed thirty years ago. You are operating in an atmosphere that emphasizes *human relations* in the handling of insurance claims. Consideration for human beings—the insured, the third-party claimant, witnesses, and all others—now is paramount.

Claims Handling Thirty Years Ago

Let us look at insurance claims adjusting thirty years ago. Adjusters were virtually all men. They wore a suit, a white shirt, a tie, and a hat, and carried a clipboard with a statement pad. Most of the time, they worked out of the office.

The statement pad was divided into original pages, alternated with carbon pages. One had to write with adequate pressure to get a good copy. Adjusters were supposed to write down everything the insured, claimant, or witness said.

The adjuster was to ask questions and attempt to put the insured's, claimant's, or witness's statements down in his or her own words in order to preserve the authenticity, accuracy, and credibility of the statement. Thus, if a witness said, "I saw the green car come down the hill, and he was going like a bat out of hell," the adjuster wrote exactly what the witness said. And if a witness said, "the rick-rack [*sic*] tore away from the side of the stream," the statement taker wrote "rick-rack," to preserve the authenticity and credibility of the witness's own words and his misuse of the English language, even though the correct term was "rip-rap."

It was highly important to preserve the witness's or claimant's exact speaking style and use or misuse of language. If the defense attorney subsequently used a statement in court to impeach or discredit the testimony of a witness, a jury would find it hard to believe a statement that was written in words and phrases that did not resemble the witness's natural manner of speaking. One could hardly lend credibility to the statement of an illiterate day laborer by transposing his poor use of English into a treatise written by a professional writer.

Today, you don't have that problem—it is all on tape. All of the warts, blemishes, and inaccuracies of everyday conversation are there. But thirty years ago, you wrote down the *witness's* statement of several pages *in his or her own words*, counted them, and wrote in conclusion, "I have read these (insert number) pages, and they are true." Then you got the witness to sign at the end of the statement and initial or sign each page on the edge of each sheet. You had to do a lot of writing.

Those were the days before man flew to the moon and before miniaturized circuits provided you with compact, reliable, portable tape recorders.

A Panorama of Human Experience Unaided by the telephone statement that is in such common use today, it was necessary for adjusters to spend most of their time in the field investigating a great variety of different claims involving a myriad of fact situations. These included inspecting construction sites, photographing physical evidence, interviewing and obtaining statements from witnesses, going to hospitals to talk to injured third-party claimants, and even visiting persons arrested for motor vehicle violations or fidelity bond matters.

The adjuster occasionally had to try to console parents immediately after the death of a small child or inform a sad, elderly couple that their only son, who had just been killed, only had medical payments insurance to cover $500 of his funeral expenses.

Sometimes when the cooperation of witnesses or claimants was in question, or the magnitude of the case required talking to many people in a short period of time, a court reporter had to be employed to accompany the adjuster on an investigation. (Statements of court reporters have great credibility in the courts, and they are useful, even today, in some claims investigations.) Most of the court reporters thirty years ago were women, and they took shorthand, rather than using the machines that are in common use today.

Adjusters witness a mixture of emotions—rage, frustration, and helplessness. A classic case is that of a man whose wife drove his new automobile into a huge construction hole, forcing her to climb out a window to escape. Obviously angry enough to strike his wife, he dismissed the idea and took his rage out on the adjuster—a typical case of *displaced aggression*.

The human drama of insurance claims handling experience— witnessing the never-ending panorama of human emotion—the pathos, the excitement, the adventure, the sense that you are dealing with real people—is an important part of the claims handling job today. It must not be lost merely because you are handling many claims by telephone. Somehow, a more personal relationship must be introduced into the telephone contact—a sense of caring, compassion, concern, consideration, and courtesy, *the five "C's" of human relations in communication.*

Five "C's" of Human Relations in Communication Caring, compassion, concern, consideration, and courtesy are required if you are to practice good human relations in communication.

Caring requires "painstaking and watchful attention" regarding the welfare of others. It involves solicitude and thoughtful attentiveness.

Compassion involves sympathy. It means sympathetic consciousness of others' distress, together with a desire to alleviate it.

Concern contemplates a marked interest or regard. The claims handling relationship creates a personal tie with others that mandates this interest in or regard for others.

Consideration combines the elements of caring, compassion, and concern. Consideration requires a thoughtful and sympathetic regard for others.

Courtesy involves respect and patience. It means that you maintain a demeanor of manners and respect without regard for circumstances that might be personally trying. It requires a behavior of allowance despite the facts. This does not mean giving away money. It means behaving in a professional, respectful, and patient manner.

There must be a projection to the person on the other end of the line that you are a warm, interested, and helpful human being, and that the insured or third-party claimant is not merely a number in a claims file. There must be an empathy with people in trouble—even though you yourself may have a burdensome workload. You must project rapport and a sense of understanding and caring. The drama of dealing with so many people in trouble and dealing with some people who are dishonest and unpleasant can harden you and make you cynical, but compassion, courtesy, and humaneness are an important part of being a successful claims adjuster.

Many people don't know what to do after a loss, and they need your immediate help and a concrete impression that *you want* to help them, that *you care* about helping them, and that *you are going to help them*. If you won't help them, an attorney will, and you may have another lawsuit on your hands.

An adjuster's concern for other humans need not compromise the insurer's economic welfare by playing "fairy godmother" with the company's money. You can be human without being foolish. Displaying good judgment requires you to protect your employer's welfare, while at the same time not ignoring the empathy, rapport, human decency, and fairness that should govern the affairs of men and women. The successful adjuster needed these qualities thirty years ago and particularly needs them now.

Privity of Contract The insurance policy is a contract. There is "privity"—a legal relation—between the insured and the insurer. Privity of contract means each owes a duty to the other. The insured must pay premiums and comply with the requirements of the policy— this includes providing assistance to and cooperating with the insurer. The insurer, in turn, owes the insured a duty of good faith in protecting the insured against losses and handling claims in an expeditious manner.

Thirty years ago, claims adjusters were taught to confine their relationship on claims to the contract. The contract always spelled out all of the responsibility of the adjuster, and it was only the insured to whom a responsibility was owed. No duty was owed a third-party claimant in contract. There was no "privity" between the insurer and a third-party claimant.

This has not changed much in most states. Theoretically, no duty is owed the claimant in contract. However, some courts have expressly or impliedly made the third-party claimant a third-party beneficiary of the insurance policy. Thus, a contractual relationship may exist. The legal philosophy behind this reasoning is that a liability insurance contract is taken out by the insured to protect third parties. Therefore, they are third-party beneficiaries under the contract.[1]

It may be difficult to understand this judicial reasoning. You may say, "The reason I buy liability insurance is to protect me if I get sued." But you must remember that the legislative intent for enacting compulsory automobile insurance laws, financial responsibility laws, and unsatisfied judgment fund statutes has been to protect the victim against the irresponsible uninsured motorist. In addition, some states require that uninsured motorists insurance be offered to every insured. Hence, the third-party beneficiary theory is not as far-fetched as it may seem at first.

Insureds as Customers   The insured and the insurance company have operated in a relationship of "privity of contract." Insureds are customers. They are entitled to the same consideration that customers of other businesses are entitled to, no more, no less.

Responsible insurance companies have always attempted to dispose of an insured's insurance claims in a timely, courteous, and considerate manner, hoping to retain the business of that insured. This, of course, has never meant sacrificing the insurance company's economic objectives.

Thirty years ago, insurance companies were not in the business of giving money away, nor are they now. Good insurance companies paid the insured the amount of money the insured was entitled to, no more and no less.

Conscientious claims people tried to expedite the insured's claim; filled out State accident report forms; and provided whatever other information they could to assist the insured. If a subrogation claim seemed appropriate, they helped the insured get back all or part of his or her deductible on automobile insurance matters. They frequently provided services "above and beyond" the contract responsibilities in order to have satisfied insureds—the customers. Whatever the nature of the case, as a matter of good business practice, the "immediate contact rule" was of primary importance to provide good service to the insured. The "immediate contact rule" is self-explanatory. It means that the adjuster must make an effort to immediately communicate and begin handling the claim.

Top insurance companies sought to provide their insureds with the best possible service, since good service was essential to retain the goodwill and the business of the insured. Occasionally, honest differences of opinion entered into the matter of the determination of liability or the extent of damages, and hard feelings sometimes arose in the course of the business. This was regrettable, but unavoidable.

In other cases, because of incompetence, alcoholism, overload, or some improper motive of the claims adjuster, insureds sometimes were not treated properly. Some adjusters were not properly trained or did not have the disposition or temperament to deal with the daily problems that confront the insurance claims adjuster, and these people sometimes projected a bad image for the insurance industry. It is also a human trait to sometimes wake up in a bad mood and carry it to the office, and a grouchy adjuster usually produces a grouchy insured.

It was not uncommon thirty years ago for most claims adjusters to devote eighteen-hour days to serious cases. Oftentimes, at "quitting time," a telephone call would summon the adjuster to the scene of an accident, and it would take several hours of investigation before the adjuster would be able to leave the case until the next day. Weekends also were not sacred and adjusters were "on call" twenty-four hours a day to respond personally, at least in major cases.

Third-Party Claimant There was no uniformity in policy regarding treatment of third-party claimants thirty years ago. Each company seemed to have its own operating philosophy regarding the treatment of the third-party claimant. The following descriptions outline two *opposite* viewpoints that were employed in the treatment of third-party claimants.

The *social responsibility viewpoint* employed by many companies dictated that claims adjusters should treat third-party claimants as human beings who were entitled to courtesy and fairness. When an insured reported an accident in which it appeared that the insured was negligent, it was standard practice to contact claimants and inform them of the procedures they should follow in order to have their claims settled.

Thus, in an automobile collision case, the claimant was advised to secure "competitive" estimates of damages. The adjuster would then examine the estimates while inspecting the automobile, and it was not uncommon for the claims adjuster to write a settlement check the same day as the automobile accident. (Before the advent of the computerized check, it was common practice for claims adjusters to carry settlement checks, and the adjuster would be authorized to settle claims up to designated limits without home office or assigning office authorization.) Many third-party claimants were considerably surprised at the fairness, courtesy, and expediency with which their claims were handled, and some third-party claimants became "tomorrow's" insureds.

The major philosophy behind using the "immediate contact rule" on third-party claimants in minor claims was that there was a duty owed to the insured under the liability insurance contract to dispose of the claim as soon as possible, thereby eliminating any possible harassment of the insured by the claimant. Serving the claimant arose out of a contractual duty to the insured. Aside from these considerations, it seemed the decent and fair thing to do.

Of course, in the case of claims that might ultimately reach the hands of an attorney because of the seriousness of personal injuries or the scope of property damage, it was always standard practice to employ the "immediate contact rule" in order to dispose of claims as economically and efficiently as possible. Then, as now, delay in serious claims usually added to the settlement value of the claim, particularly after an attorney was employed by the claimant. Good sense always dictated that claimants be contacted immediately in these cases so that settlement overtures might be made promptly. Where a settlement was not immediately possible, it was most important for the adjuster to maintain constant communication with the claimant, thereby assuring the claimant of cooperation and forestalling the entry of a plaintiff's attorney.

The other extreme in the handling of third-party matters was to treat the claimant as an adversary to whom no responsibility was owed. This attitude may be called the *anti-social viewpoint*. There was a solid body of legal thought that supported this viewpoint. After all, the third-party claimant had no privity of contract with the insurance company; therefore, no contractual duty was owed to the claimant. There was no statute or insurance department rule or regulation that dictated that third-party claimants were to be treated with courtesy or fairness. Furthermore, payment of claims aggravated the loss ratio.

Thus, the objective was to treat the claimant as an adversary, the enemy, throwing impediments in his or her path. Courtesy and fairness were irrelevant. In extreme cases, claims departments were instructed to deny all third-party claims, regardless of merit. It was well known that some of the claimants would not bother to secure the services of an attorney, thus these claims would not have to be paid and would reflect favorably on the loss ratio of the company. This technique, of course, was primarily used on property damage claims and minor bodily injury claims.

Therefore, with the anti-social viewpoint concerning a third-party claimant, the policy was one of no cooperation, no contact, and deliberate delay of the claim, thus forcing the claimant to the point of suit. If he or she sued on a simple property damage claim, further delay and lack of cooperation frequently resulted in a compromise settlement which resulted in partial payment to the claimant, and saved the insurance company money.

Serious bodily injury liability claims were another matter. Even the most hard-hearted insurance companies believed in the prudence of the "immediate contact rule" in the case of serious bodily injury cases or in claims of such magnitude that the entry of an attorney seemed to be imminent if the claims department engaged in dilatory tactics.

The social responsibility viewpoint in the treatment of third-party claimants stresses:

1. the "immediate contact rule"—making a prompt effort to handle the claim;
2. communication—this, too, must be timely, for it is part of the "immediate contact rule." Good communication also contemplates continuing communication with the claimant so that the latter does not begin to feel ignored or betrayed;
3. courtesy—claimants are entitled to courteous and helpful attention. Although, traditionally, claimants have been consid-

ered to be strangers to the contract, they should not be treated as "the enemy"—as adversaries;

4. fairness and honesty—there is no place for dishonesty and "sharp practice" in the social responsibility viewpoint. The adjuster is not expected to compromise the insurer's defensive position in the handling of a claim, but fairness and honest behavior in business has been a hallmark of British and American commercial law for centuries.

There is no room in insurance claims handling today for the anti-social viewpoint. It was a poor viewpoint thirty years ago, and it is a catastrophic concept today. The behavior manifest in the anti-social school of claims adjusting is illegal in some jurisdictions and dangerous, at best, in the remaining jurisdictions.

Claims Handling Practices Today

In the past thirty years, great changes have occurred in the area of insurance claims handling and in the conduct of interviews and other factors of claims handling investigations. These have been brought about by the revolution in recording technology, which now makes it possible for claims representatives to handle most claims by telephone, thus preserving the facts and evidence of the case by the use of a recording device.

Most insurance claims offices are equipped with desk recorders, and telephone recorders are in constant use by many insurance company claims departments, independent adjusters, and large insurance adjusting firms. Portable tape recorders are utilized outside the office. It is not uncommon for some companies to handle a major portion of their claims by telephone. In many cases, the claims adjuster never steps out of the office. It is probably accurate to state that most insurance companies today utilize the telephone as the principal tool in claims handling and investigation.

Focus on Cutting Claims Expenses Insurance companies have been accused in recent years of abandoning the insurance business. Many companies, harassed by the political interference with ratemaking and with loss and expense ratios that exceed 100 percent, have relied principally upon interest earnings on prepaid premiums in order to make a profit. These profit margins have dwindled as interest rates have declined during the mid-1980s.

It is contended that the property and liability industry, responding to the problem of high loss ratios, has appeared to confront the problem with a reduction and consolidation of claims operations. By cutting claims handling expenses, companies have hoped to provide for more efficient business operations. The result of this approach has been to expect claims adjusters or claims examiners to handle case loads of as many as 500 or 600 files efficiently. This situation has become more and more common as cost cutting, office consolidations, and reorganizations have continued throughout industry claims operations.[2]

From a bottom-line, cost-reduction perspective, this approach has appeared to produce operational savings. Claims departments have been pushed to handle more claims faster and with fewer resources. To handle the increased volume of claims assigned to individual adjusters, greater emphasis has been placed upon telephone and mail claims service.

"Outside" Adjusters   Because of the new recording technology, an interesting dichotomy of claims adjuster organization has developed. There are "outside" adjusters, and "inside" adjusters. The "outside" adjusters are typically the more experienced individuals who operate much the same as the adjuster of thirty years ago except that they are now armed with portable tape recorders rather than with statement pads. The outside adjuster handles those cases in which it appears that a face-to-face approach is indicated.

For example, when the insured appears to be liable for the accident, it is often appropriate for the adjuster to visit the hospital room of a badly injured third-party claimant to talk to that individual and his or her family. The adjuster displays sympathy and rapport with the family, promises to take care of all medical bills while the individual is hospitalized, offers to make advance payments to take care of family expenses while the individual is unable to contribute to the family income, and makes other necessary arrangements. This kind of person-to-person contact is highly essential to insure the other party that there is a sincere interest on the part of the insurance company.

It is difficult to do an adequate job of fraud investigation, particularly in arson cases, if one is sitting at a desk all of the time. In October 1984, the All-Industry Research Advisory Council published the results of a survey on insurance company use of Special Investigative Units for fraud investigations. Sixteen insurers who were able to provide both program costs and estimated savings reported an average savings in claims costs of $7.39 for every dollar invested in a Special Investigative Unit. These units were made up primarily of people who operated out in the field. In the case of suspected arson, it is essential to make an on-site investigation to determine the origin of the fire, to interrogate witnesses regarding the smell or the appearance of the fire, and to check for any incendiary devices that may have been the cause of the fire. Premises must be examined to see whether evidence exists that a barebones inventory was in the building at the time of the fire, and whether more valuable items had been removed prior to the occurrence. This, of course, could not be accomplished by telephone.

In addition, of course, there are many other cases where a telephone call is not sufficient. Adjusters who go out and inspect storm damage and handle catastrophe windstorm or flood damages obviously must inspect the damages. They can conclude claims much faster if they are on the scene of the catastrophe. These claims cannot be handled by telephone.

Personal contact, on-site inspections of damage, and street investigations, are necessary to establish rapport and communication with both insureds and third-party claimants in many such situations. They cannot be accomplished by telephone. These personal contacts do much to accomplish a positive consumer attitude. Consequently, it is the opinion of experienced claims people that personal contact contributes enormously to a decrease in litigation.

"Inside" Adjusters   Outside investigations seem to be mandatory in many types of insurance claims; yet economic expediency has relegated many claims to the telephone. The emphasis is upon volume disposition of insurance claims, and anything that can be handled by telephone is assigned to "inside" adjusters.

However, the role of the "inside" adjuster cannot be trivialized. There are hosts of simple claims situations that can be rapidly and economically disposed of by telephone without the adjuster's ever leaving the office. This has always been the case.

In addition, telephone recordings, if taken correctly, can serve as adequate evidential material. These recordings, if used in court, may be more persuasive than written statements of the past in influencing judges and juries.

Statements can be taken from insureds, third-party claimants, and witnesses regarding accidents or loss situations, and these can serve as adequate materials upon which to base an investigation report for purposes of reporting to the home office or the assigning office. Further, by telephone assignment, photographers can be employed to photograph accident sites or damaged properties, contractors can be contacted to provide estimates or begin repairs; and many other functions can be adequately served by telephone communication. Again, this was true thirty years ago.

The charge is sometimes made that a telephone conversation is cold and impersonal. This is certainly true in many cases; however, it is often not the fault of the telephone but, rather, of the telephone personality of the claims adjuster. Many "inside" adjusters, like telephone personnel in a host of other fields, are able to project warmth, understanding, and sympathy in a telephone conversation. Telephone manners, courtesy, and a projection of warmth can be accomplished most competently by "inside" adjusters. If the telephone conversation appears to be cold and impersonal, it is the fault of the caller rather than of the telephone.

The telephone, in fact, offers some distinct advantages in the handling of insurance claims. There is nothing that infuriates an insured or a third-party claimant more than the feeling that a just claim is being ignored by an insurance company. "Inside" insurance adjusters today, while confined to the office and skilled in telephone use, have the capability of making much more frequent contact than did the claims adjuster of thirty years ago.

Unburdened by the time constraints of travel or personal face-to-face contact "outside," there is the potential for "inside" adjusters to make many more contacts today. The claims adjuster who is skilled in good telephone manners and courtesy, and who projects sympathy and good rapport, is able to keep up a continual contact with the insured or third-party claimant by making frequent telephone calls to report on the progress of claims.

One should note, however, that adjusters had telephones thirty years ago and were able to keep a constant line of communication open with the other party, as well as make face-to-face contacts. In those days, however, the telephone was used to secure information, but one did not use the telephone to secure evidential materials. Thus, there was no reliance placed upon the telephone for those purposes, and there wasn't as much time to use the telephone, because the adjuster was outside the office gathering evidence.

TODAY'S PERILOUS WORLD OF CLAIMS ADJUSTING

A marked legal revolution has occurred in the world of insurance claims adjusting during the past thirty years. Some authors call it a "revolution of rising entitlements." Through education, through more widespread emphasis upon consumer protection, and because of a new philosophy regarding the individual's relationships with large institutions, the individual has developed an expectancy of fair play and a belief in the legal doctrine of "caveat venditor" (let the seller beware).

The term, "revolution of rising entitlements," refers to the fact that people expect more of large institutions, government, and their own legal rights. "I exist. Therefore, I am entitled," is a common viewpoint among the public today. As one authority points out:

> This is an age of discontent, of skepticism, and of challenge to established authority. Today's consumers are much better educated

than those of the past, and they challenge practices that previous generations bore in silence. They question the authority of the uncontrolled market place.[3]

Because of this "revolution of rising entitlements," we have new statutes, new case decisions, a new philosophy, and new mandatory claims procedures that must be understood by the insurance adjuster of today.

Among the problems that confront today's adjuster are expectations regarding his or her conduct which were never dreamed of thirty years ago. In some states, new statutes have been enacted that create extracontractual rights of action for insureds and third-party claimants—these are the unfair claims settlement practices statutes.

New court decisions have expanded the rights of consumers (both insureds and third-party claimants) beyond the expectations of even some of the legislatures that enacted the new laws. Policy monetary limitations under a variety of different policies are routinely exceeded in court cases where an allegation of "bad faith" charged against the insurance company and its personnel, primarily the claims adjuster, is proven. In a number of cases, bad faith has been evidenced by simple negligence, suggesting that one may not be able to afford to make any human mistakes in the handling of insurance claims.

Even more dangerous is to take personally comments made by an insured or a third-party claimant. You must always "keep your cool." In other words, you must not display any form of emotion or act in a way that would suggest that you are being arbitrary, capricious, or abusive because of hostility toward the other individual. You must always realize that people who have just experienced a loss frequently suffer physical and psychological stress; and it is not uncommon for them to direct their frustration and anger toward an adjuster.

To resent such displays of anger is only human; however, you must always refrain from engaging in conduct that would show anger or a lack of professionalism. With the rise in volume of litigation, juries are always interested and aware of any manifestation of hostility or lack of control on the part of claims adjusters that might be construed to be the basis for an arbitrary and capricious denial of a claim or prejudicial handling of a claim. This can land you right in the middle of a "bad faith" lawsuit in which you, personally, can be held partly responsible for any damages awarded to the insured or the third-party claimant. If your perceived misconduct is considered to be particularly reprehensible by the jury, you can also be assessed punitive damages for your behavior. Much of this may not make sense to you; however, it is very much a fact of life in the field of insurance claims adjusting today.

Opening Your Claims File

Thirty years ago we did not have to worry about having our insurance investigation files subject to court and jury scrutiny. As a matter of fact, merely mentioning in court the fact that an insurance company was actually defending an insured could be held prejudicial and improper.

In such a case, the judge would dismiss the jury, and the case would start all over again, necessitating the impaneling of a new jury. The rule seemed to be absurd because most people knew that an insurance company was involved in most of the lawsuits. Today, however, we have insureds and third-party claimants suing the insurance company directly and sometimes suing the claims adjuster as well, and it is perfectly proper to mention the fact that an insurance company is involved, since it is the defendant.

Right of "Discovery" In addition, the plaintiff insured or third-party claimant has a rather liberalized right of "discovery." The plaintiff's attorneys will do anything possible to acquire your investigation file, which usually contains witnesses' statements, photographs, inter-office communications and the investigator's own evaluation of the case in question. The right of discovery has existed for a long time, and it has been common in many states in the past to be able to obtain copies of witnesses' statements and photographs, but the insurer's own inter-office communications and personal evaluations of a particular claim were immune from the discovery privilege of the plaintiff, often by reference to the *"Work Product Rule."* This rule essentially provides that any materials in the investigation file prepared in anticipation of litigation are privileged and immune from discovery. The work product rule is derived from Rule 26 of the Federal Rules of Civil Procedure. Rule 26 provides:

(1) In General. Parties may obtain discovery regarding any matter, not privileged, which is relevant to the subject matter involved in the pending action...

(3) Trial Preparation: Materials ... (A) party may obtain discovery of documents and tangible things otherwise discoverable under subdivision (b) (1) of this rule and prepared in anticipation of litigation or for trial by or for another party or by or for that other party's representative ... only upon showing that the party seeking discovery has substantial need of the materials in the preparation of his case and that he is unable without undue hardship to obtain the substantial equivalent of the materials by other means. In ordering discovery of such materials when the required showing has been made, the court shall protect against disclosure of the mental impressions, conclusions, opinions, or legal theories of an attorney or other representative of a party concerning the litigation.

In one case, an insurer denied coverage to its insured, although well aware there was indeed coverage. Its claims manager wrote in an internal memo "lets [sic] bluff it out we can always buy out at a later date."[4] This mental impression or conclusion of the claims manager would appear to have fallen within the ideas expressed in Rule 26; however, the court determined that it was not a privileged communication and consequently served as an excellent bit of evidence for the jury to substantiate a "bad faith" recovery against the insurance company and the claims manager.

Most states have adopted a work product rule that is identical to or substantially similar to the federal rule.[5] The federal courts and the courts in most states recognize that there are two different types of work product: (1) "factual" work product and (2) "opinion" work product.

"Factual" work product encompasses the claim investigator's witness statements and photographs. To discover such materials, a party must show a substantial need for the materials and establish the inability to otherwise obtain substantially equivalent materials without undue hardship. An even stronger need is required for disclosure of "opinion" work product, which is material containing the investigator's or attorney's mental impressions, conclusions, opinions, or legal theories.

Hair and Pulignano's article points out that the "need" or "substantial need" requirement necessary to overcome work product immunity is normally met by showing:

1. the documents contained crucial information in the exclusive control of the opposing party;
2. the information is not as readily available to the moving party as the opposing party; or
3. withholding the information and the documents sought would defeat the interests of justice.[6]

Courts make a distinction between those materials collected in "anticipation of litigation" and those materials collected in "the ordinary course of business." The former are immune from discovery, while the latter must be revealed to the opposing party on request. Although you may believe that all of your investigation is directed toward the possible anticipation of litigation, many courts do not take this position.

The "ordinary course of business" for an insurance company is the anticipation of litigation; however, courts have insisted that attorneys be consulted or be involved in order to classify any documents as having been prepared "in anticipation of litigation." Therefore, your evidential materials, including the evaluation of what you believe to be routine claims, are not considered as ordinarily undertaken in anticipation of litigation. This is the case even though litigation often does result from such claims. Reports emanating from initial or early investigative activities by the insurance adjuster are typically discoverable. This includes your notes and investigative reports and the usual statements of opinion that you present in writing to your home office or assigning office.

Courts will look to the "uniqueness" of the material sought and the potential hardship to the plaintiff should he or she be denied discovery. If your mental impressions and personal evaluations written into your investigative report show any indication that you have acted in a prejudicial, unfair, or arbitrary manner, or if there is anything else in your behavior to suggest a violation of unfair claims practices requirements, you are most certain to have your impressions and evaluations appear in a court of law when the plaintiff brings suit alleging misconduct.

Discovery is usually denied by courts in cases where litigation was pending or imminent at the time you prepared the report. In addition, if an attorney is actively involved in the case when you prepared the report, discovery is usually denied. The plaintiff must also show "substantial need" for the document or "undue hardship" if production is not allowed. However, you cannot rely on the work product rule to protect you in every case, since the courts are becoming more liberal in providing discovery privileges.

Of course, the attorney-client privilege is absolute in most cases. Certain basic elements must be proved, however, in order to claim the attorney-client privilege:

1. The asserted holder of the privilege is or has sought to become a client;
2. The person to whom the communication was made
   a. is a member of a bar or a court, or is a subordinate, and
   b. in connection with this communication is acting as a lawyer;
3. The communication relates to a fact of which the attorney was informed
   a. by his client
   b. without the presence of strangers
   c. for the purposes of securing primarily either
      i. an opinion on law or
      ii. legal service or
      iii. assistance in some legal proceeding, and
   d. not for the purpose of committing a crime or tort; and
4. The privilege has been

      a. claimed and

      b. not waived by the client.[7]

Exception—No Defense in Bad Faith Cases   You have *no* defense against discovery demands in actions against insurance companies based on their alleged bad faith in dealing with their insureds. The work product immunity and the attorney-client privilege rule *do not* apply. All state courts that have addressed the issue have required the companies to produce their claims files up to and including the date of judgment in the original litigation, even though the file contains mental impressions and "opinion" work product.

The courts have ruled that by the very nature of bad faith claims, the "substantial need" requirement is met.[8] The federal courts, similarly, do not recognize the work product immunity on bad faith cases.

Significance of "Work Product Rule" to You   You should not derive particular comfort from the fact that there might be such a thing as a "work product rule." It does not protect you in "bad faith" cases. Stick to the facts and make certain that every written statement made by you, every impression that you have regarding a claim, and every evaluation that you transmit in writing reflects concrete facts that you have discovered.

Make certain that your written impressions and communications clearly portray honesty, fairness, and reasonableness. Every time you send a letter or an investigation report to your home office or assigning office, and every time you place a written statement in your claims file, think lawsuit. Always be aware that this material may be used in court in some future case and that your words will be read to a jury or to a judge. Practice "aggressive good faith" in all of your communications, particularly those that are written and subject to discovery.

New Statutes on Claims Handling

Most of the states have now enacted "Unfair Claims Settlement Practices Acts." These state laws spell out the rules of misconduct that can subject claims adjusters together with their employers to legal liability in cases brought by insureds as well as third-party claimants. Quite likely, you have a statute in your state that mandates the method by which you must handle claims.

These laws typically require that you make immediate contact, that you maintain communication with insureds and third-party claimants, and that you conclude claims in a timely manner. These statutes require you to practice "aggressive good faith" and to make "prompt, fair, and equitable settlements of claims in which liability has become reasonably clear."

If you fail to follow the many new mandates of the state laws or the rules and regulations prescribed by your state insurance department, you will most likely end up with a claim brought against your employer and possibly against you. This may take the form of a complaint directed to the state insurance department, or a suit for bad faith, even including punitive damages in some jurisdictions.

The subject of the Unfair Claims Settlement Practices statutes is described in detail in a later chapter. Make certain that you thoroughly study the rules that mandate your expected behavior. This is the only way to stay out of court.

The Legal Climate—A Changing Scene

It has always been the responsibility of claims adjusters to try to keep claims out of court. Adjusters have always been instructed to avoid having a case go to attorneys, because it is well known that once an attorney takes a case, the cost of the claim escalates. There is a simple reason for this. Attorneys must justify their value to their clients; consequently, they are likely to refuse to settle for the amount you have previously offered to an insured or a third-party claimant. This is frequently the case, even though you have made an absolutely fair settlement offer to the other party. This was true thirty years ago, but today the problem has worsened measurably. There are a number of reasons for this.

Increase in Attorneys The United States has more lawyers per capita than any nation in the world. Law schools in the past several decades have been turning out record numbers of lawyers, all of whom are trying to make a living. The more attorneys, it seems, the more lawsuits, and insurance companies are becoming more and more involved in litigation.

In addition, developments on the federal level have contributed to the increase in litigation. Thirty years ago attorneys were not permitted to advertise. Since then, however, the federal anti-trust laws have been applied to the legal profession, as well as to other professions, and the canons of legal ethics that governed an attorney's behavior have been interpreted to be anti-competitive with respect to advertising restrictions as well as to minimum fee schedules. Consequently, attorneys now advertise more openly in writing. They place fee information in the windows of their offices. Some advertise aggressively on television and have even opened thirty-minute free legal clinics in flea markets. Many attorneys are scrambling for business, and they are using novel techniques in order to acquire it.

Anyone who has been in the insurance claims adjusting field for very long is aware that some attorneys engage in "ambulance chasing," a practice that is prohibited by law and legal ethics. Nevertheless, it is a fact of life, and today it is more prevalent than ever before.

More Litigation   Many writers and spokesmen on this subject contend that there is a "litigation explosion." Others disagree. Researcher Marc Galanter at the University of Wisconsin Law School states: "If you count cases per capita, there are not unprecedented levels." According to the National Center for State Courts, the volume of civil cases filed in state courts jumped sharply compared with the population increase between 1978 and 1981, but it then leveled off to about 15 million annually.

However, former Chief Justice Burger of the U.S. Supreme Court stated in May of 1986 that civil cases of all kinds filed in federal district courts continued to increase at a rate far above population growth. He reported that in the past decade the number of tort cases filed in federal court increased 62 percent from 25,691 to 41,593. This included a 370 percent increase, from 2,886 to 13,554, in products-liability cases in which products—from cars to can openers—were blamed for injuries.

Thirty years ago there were only half a dozen states in the United States that recognized the theory of comparative negligence in tort awards. Contributory negligence was the main standard followed; and if plaintiffs were in *any* degree responsible for their misfortune, they could not recover from others. Today, contributory negligence does not dissuade plaintiffs from bringing lawsuits. Almost all states use the comparative negligence standard. Plaintiffs are aware of the fact that a lenient jury or judge may award them sizable awards under the doctrine of comparative negligence, even if they were partly responsible.

There have been some major victories for plaintiffs even when they have been largely at fault for their own misfortunes. For example, in April of 1985 a jury in a California state court awarded damages to the widow and two children of a man who was electrocuted when the 28-foot mast of his catamaran boat struck overhead electric wires while he was carrying the boat to a trailer on the beach. Although the jury found the victim to be 37.5 percent responsible for his own death, it awarded the widow and children $515,000 against the catamaran company and the electric company, and $1.4 million in punitive damages against the catamaran company because of reports of similar injuries from the aluminum masts. The company has since re-designed the masts so that they do not conduct electricity.

There are many targets of litigation. Cities are being sued for everything from unfilled potholes to police misconduct; corporate officers and directors find themselves as defendants in a wide variety of securities-law claims; employers are in court justifying hiring and firing policies; lawyers, architects, and accountants have joined the ranks of professions sued for malpractice; and even the actions of state judges can now be challenged when they go beyond the judge's legal authority and official duties. The risk of liability from automobile accidents and a host of other liability situations swells the number of lawsuits that have resulted.

Although it would appear that people and attorneys today are more contentious and more inclined to go to court, it is not a universal belief. One of the most celebrated jurists of the present century, Learned Hand, cautioned that "as a litigant, I should dread a lawsuit beyond almost anything else short of sickness and death." Attorneys are taught in law school to try to keep their clients out of trouble. As former Chief Justice Warren Burger stated in 1985, he was taught that "the highest obligation of a lawyer to his client was to keep the client out of the courtroom if possible." After hearing a report presented to the National Association of Attorney Generals that said there is no lawsuit crisis or "profitability crisis in the insurance industry," Attorney General Jim Mattox of Texas declared that insurance companies are engaged in one of the "most insidious conspiratorial frauds that I've ever seen in the free world." The insurance industry has disputed the report's findings.

Support for the U.S. insurance industry's viewpoint comes from England. Lloyd's of London now requires that all its liability policies written in the U.S. be underwritten on a "claims-made" basis. Some 100 Lloyd's underwriters were threatened with bankruptcy in 1985 because of their U.S. business. This prompted Lloyd's Chairman Peter Miller to declare in September of 1985: "Virtually all our losses come from [the U.S.], which generates 12 percent of our income. As a businessman, I say to myself, 'Why carry on?' "

Higher Jury Awards According to a study conducted by the risk management firm of Tillinghast, Nelson, and Warren, tort claims and lawyers' fees in 1984 represented 1.76 percent of the Gross National Product, and liability costs have increased 61 percent since 1980. Jury Verdict Research, Inc., an Ohio company, reported that between 1980 and 1984 the number of jury awards of $1 million or more jumped nearly 200 percent, to 401. Some cases are bizarre. A Philadelphia jury in March of 1986 awarded $988,000 to a woman who said a CAT scan had caused her to lose her psychic power. While many large jury awards are reduced or reversed on appeal, the trend toward increased awards is indisputable.

There is considerable controversy over whether there is indeed a liability crisis or that the resultant increase in litigation is bad. Consumer groups and plaintiffs' lawyers say that the crisis, such as it is, has been created by liability insurers raising their rates astronomically and unnecessarily. They also point out that statistics on jury verdicts often are incomplete and do not take into account awards that are reduced or thrown out on appeal.

Ralph Nader, a critic of the insurance industry, questions whether "verdicts and awards have done anything more than barely keep up with inflation." He contends that the insurance industry "is trying to generate a revolution and reduction of the rights of injured people."

Nevertheless, national attention has been focused on what has been characterized as a "liability crisis." Critics such as Victor Schwartz, a Washington attorney and former law professor, contend that "tort law used to be based on fault. Now, it is asked by courts to do something that was never intended—to be a system for compensating all injuries, without regard for who's right and wrong."

New Restrictive Laws Enacted Some states are now restricting the amount of recovery a plaintiff can receive for pain and suffering. Twenty states had enacted such limitations in the first eight months of 1986. In addition, states are imposing laws that restrict the fee an attorney may charge. In general, the new laws allow the traditional fees for prosecuting minor lawsuits but reduce them sharply for large cases involving serious injuries. Eleven states had enacted legislation curbing contingency fees in the first eight months of 1986.

New York, for example, limits fees in medical and dental malpractice cases to 30 percent of the first $250,000 recovered, 25 percent of the next $250,000, 20 percent of the next $500,000, 15 percent of the next $250,000, and 10 percent of any amount over $1,250,000. The aim is "to reduce the incentive to push for ever higher and higher verdicts, and for more of the verdict to end up with the injured person."

A great deal of attention has been devoted on the national legislative level to the subject of the "liability problem." A number of bills have been introduced in Congress to restrict the amount of recovery plaintiffs may receive in liability suits, particularly in products liability cases. However, no legislation had been enacted by late 1986.

Joint and Several Liability The subject of joint and several liability is of great interest to every claims adjuster. The doctrine specifies that when two or more individuals are jointly responsible for a tort (they are called joint tortfeasors), an injured plaintiff can recover from any or all of the responsible persons up to the amount of the plaintiff's damages. As a consequence, the phenomenon known as "deep pockets" developed. It typically arises where one of the defendants, usually a large corporation with a great deal of financial resources, and another less affluent individual defendant, are jointly responsible for a plaintiff's damages. Typically, the plaintiff focuses on the large corporation to recover damages, since the corporation has "deep pockets"—great ability to pay—even though it may be considerably less liable for plaintiff's damages than the individual defendant who is found to be more responsible but who has few resources—little ability to pay.

Because of new legislation in a number of states the doctrine of joint and several liability has been revised now so that it does not apply in liability cases. Instead of having an indivisible responsibility, several states have now specified that each party responsible for a tort will be allocated the respective percentage of fault and at least with respect to intangible damages, such as pain and suffering, will be responsible only for a portion of the damages awarded to the plaintiff. In the first eight months of 1986, some fifteen states had enacted laws that affect the doctrine of joint and several liability.

The variations in legislation differ substantially in those states with new laws. The following three states illustrate that variety. California in 1986 passed legislation making it so that defendants will now pay only their actual percentage of fault for noneconomic damages. Alaska enacted a law which specifies that defendants who have less than 50 percent fault do not have to pay more than twice the amount of their culpability. Connecticut, likewise, passed a law in 1986 that holds defendants closer to their actual degree of fault. We can expect additional states to enact laws modifying or eliminating the doctrine.

Significance of the New Laws to You   The significance of this development to you is that if you are found guilty of an unfair claims settlement practice or bad faith, you may be apportioned a larger percentage of the fault and be required to pay your respective share of any judgment that is awarded should your employer fail to do so. This can have serious implications for you, since you will be required for your own welfare to carry huge amounts of liability coverage or face the possible loss of virtually all of your assets.

SUMMARY

It should be abundantly clear to you at this point that there is a perilous world of claims adjusting out there. In the day-to-day operations of claims departments, each practitioner must be fully aware of the consequences of not performing his or her job in a proper manner.

Education is the key to surviving in this perilous world. You must know the rules that must be followed in proper claims practice. You must be familiar with the statutes and the insurance department rules and regulations that govern how you perform your job. You must employ good human relations in claims adjusting.

If you conduct most of your work by telephone, you must inject a personal relationship into the telephone contact—a sense of caring, compassion, concern, consideration, and courtesy—*the five "C's" of good human relations in communication.* You must show the people with whom you come in contact that you definitely want to help them, that you care about helping them, and that you are going to help them. You must practice "aggressive good faith." You must stay out of court.

The failure to practice "aggressive good faith" will produce potentially unfavorable and highly detrimental results for you. Poor performance will result in an adverse job rating for you. You may find yourself looking for another job. Your future is at stake.

Poor performance can land you in court, defending your conduct on the job. You can be "raked over the coals" for bad faith conduct and be subjected to disciplinary action by your state insurance department or to financial liability by the courts.

You can subject your insurance company to legal liability, and you, personally, can be held responsible for money damages arising out of your conduct. You must practice "aggressive good faith" and stay out of court.

Chapter Notes

1. *Thompson v. Commercial Union Insurance Company of New York*, 250 S. 2d 259 at 261 (1971 Fla.).
2. Frederic H. Martin, "Claims Investigation: A Cost-Cutting Casualty?" *Risk Management* (June 1986), p. 18.
3. George A. Steiner and John F. Steiner, *Business, Government and Society*, 4th ed. (New York: Random House Business Division, 1985), p. 440.
4. *Farris v. United States Fidelity and Guaranty Co.*, 587 P.2d 1015 at 1016 (1978).
5. Mattox S. Hair and Nicholas V. Pulignano, Jr., "Discovery of the Insurance Investigator's Claim File," *For The Defense* (January, 1986); see *The Adjuster's Report* (Summer 1986), p. 17.
6. Hair and Pulignano, p. 17.
7. In Re Grand Jury Proceedings, *United States v. Jones*, 517 F.2d 666, at 670 (5th Cir. 1970).
8. Hair and Pulignano, p. 21.

CHAPTER 2

Bad Faith

In every contract there is an implied covenant of good faith and fair dealing that neither party will do anything which impairs the right of the other to receive the benefits of the agreement. This principle is applicable to policies of insurance.[1]

RATIONALE AND DEFINITION

The words "bad faith" are actually an imprecise label for what is essentially some kind of unreasonable conduct. The concept of good faith rises out of a duty implied because of the nature of the insurance contract itself. By the terms of this contract, the right and duty to defend the insured is granted to the insurer, giving it exclusive control over claims negotiations and settlement and the conduct of litigation. The insured is excluded from any interference in any negotiations for settlement or legal procedure.[2] This has been a reasonable arrangement giving rights and privileges that are necessary for the insurer to have in order to justify or enable it to assume the obligations which it owes to the insured by contract of insurance.

However, where an injury occurs for which a recovery may be had in a sum exceeding the amount of the insurance, the insured may become exposed to personal liability. At this point, a duty of good faith on the part of the insurer to the insured may especially come into focus, because the insured has given the insurance company all the rights that the insured possessed to protect himself or herself from the consequences of claims and litigation.

Since the insurer has taken over the duty of protecting the insured, and the contract prohibits the insured from settling, or negotiating for a settlement, or interfering in any manner except upon the request of

25

the insurer, the insurance company must undertake these responsibilities and rights in good faith.

James H. Donaldson, in his book *Casualty Claim Practice*, defines bad faith as follows:

> Bad faith. Generally implying or involving actual or constructive fraud, or a design to mislead or deceive another, or a neglect or a refusal to fulfill some duty or some contractual obligation; not prompted by an honest mistake as to one's rights or duties, but by some interested or sinister motive. It differs from the negative idea of *negligence* in that it contemplates a state of mind affirmatively operating within a furtive design or some motive of interest or ill will.[3]

While the inclusion of the word "neglect" would seem to imply negligence, it is ruled out further in the definition. Most courts have based liability upon the factors of "insincerity, dishonesty, disloyalty, duplicity, or deceitful conduct; it implies dishonesty, fraud or concealment.[4] Bad faith "requires an extraordinary showing of disingenuous or dishonest failure to carry out a contract."[5] It depends upon the general attitude and conduct of an insurer and obviously should require more than mere negligence or bad judgment. As one court observed, "the gift of prophecy has never been bestowed on ordinary mortals."[6] We will see later in this chapter that negligence is not an alien consideration in a bad faith action.

A Fiduciary Responsibility

The nature of the insurance contract, where the insured turns over his or her financial interests to the insurance company, dictates that the insurer has no right to sacrifice those of the insured in order to save money. The relationship between the insured and the insurer under the contract closely approximates that of principal and agent, or beneficiary and trustee, and indeed, some courts have held that the insurer occupies a fiduciary position.

Contract and Tort Liability

The good faith responsibility of insurers has reached the point where there is an *extra-contractual duty of good faith* so that a bad faith act can both breach the insurance contract *and* violate a statute. It is well established that violations of duty created by law—either common law or statute—can give rise to a cause of action in tort.

Thus, a majority of states now hold that an insured may have a right to recover extra-contractual damages against his or her insurer for the tort of what is commonly described as "bad faith." Increasingly the breach of good faith has become the source of spectacular jury awards.

EARLY HISTORY OF BAD FAITH

Ironically, it appears that the insurance industry was the author of its own misfortune by introducing the subject of bad faith to the law. In the 1914 New York case of *Brassil v. Maryland Casualty Co.*, there was a wrongful refusal to represent the insured who sought to appeal an adverse judgment.[7] The defendant insurance company carried employers liability insurance on the plaintiff. (This was before workers compensation.) The policy, dated June 1899, carried a $1,500 limit of liability for any one employee. A youth named Loughlin (under age twenty-one) was injured, and he and his father sued the employer. The Loughlins offered to settle for $1,500, and the employer urged the insurer to settle on that basis. The insurer believed the amount to be excessive and elected to defend the action. The Loughlins were given a judgment of over $6,000 against the employer.

The employer wished to appeal the judgment, but the insurer believed it would be useless and refused to appeal. The insurer wrote a letter to the employer, stating that the insurer "holds itself ready to comply with the terms of its contract with you in case you should satisfy the judgment rendered against you." It further signified its willingness to permit the employer to substitute his own attorney to prosecute on appeal. The employer replied that since the insurer's refusal to settle for $1,500 inflicted a much greater liability on the employer, the latter would hold the insurer liable for the full amount.

The employer's appeal was successful. He then sued the insurer for expenses and attorney's fees and recovered. The insurer in its defense relied on the policy language that gave it exclusive control over claims negotiations and settlement and any legal proceeding, declaring that it was incumbent upon the insured employer to "deal fairly and in good faith" with the insurance company. The court retorted that it was not less the "correlative obligation" of the insurance company to "deal fairly and in good faith" with the insured. The court declared that underlying all written agreements is the "obligation of good faith in carrying out what is written."

This case appears to be the origin of the doctrine of good faith.[8] Remarkably, this doctrine of good faith and its antithesis, "bad faith," which have caused the insurance industry such distress, were introduced by an insurance company back in 1914.

Although the concept of bad faith was introduced by the courts early in the twentieth century, insurance contracts were strictly construed by the courts in those years, and Brassil v. Maryland Casualty Company seemed to be an anomaly in the law for some time. The insurer was considered to have complete freedom to settle a claim or refuse to settle it in virtually all cases. Indeed, in New York, in 1923, a court declared:

> There is nothing in the policy by which the insurance company obligated itself to settle if an opportunity presented itself. It was given the option to settle, if it saw fit to do so or to try the action as it preferred. It, however, was under no legal obligation, either express or implied, to compromise or settle the claims prior to the trial.[9]

For years during the early part of the twentieth century many courts took the position that the insurer was free to settle or not as it saw fit. The only obligation of the insurer was to defend and pay within the policy limits. This, however, was not to be the modern view relating to good faith conduct under the insurance contract.

MODERN BAD FAITH LAW

The legal philosophy of the early part of the twentieth century was soon to give way to modern bad faith law. Public expectations created a change in the courts, and the modern philosophy regarding "bad faith" emerged.

Perhaps the turning point in bad faith law was the 1957 landmark decision of *Brown v. Guarantee Insurance Company*.[10] In this case, the insurer was viewed as fiduciary, owing the insured a duty to exercise good faith in cases where the insurer engages in compromise negotiations of a claim against an insured.

Some authors trace the beginning of the bad faith tort (rather than contract) doctrine to a 1973 California case.[11] However, the Brown case (also in California) was decided on the basis of tort liability, since "the insurance contract in the instant case is not before the court...."[12] Besides establishing a tort right of action, the Brown case is particularly important in providing a broad discussion of the doctrine of bad faith and enumerating a number of possible factors which might contribute to bad faith determination.

Factors Contributing to Bad Faith

Factors which might contribute to bad faith are enumerated in the Brown decision. They include the following:

1. attempts by the insurer to induce insured to contribute to settlement;
2. failure to investigate;

3. rejection of attorney's advice;
4. failure to inform the insured of an offer;
5. amount of financial risk to both parties; and
6. fault of insured in inducing insurer to reject offer by misleading it as to the facts.

These factors are all important today, and they warrant discussion.

Inducing Insured to Contribute Where an insurer attempts to obtain contribution from an insured to a settlement *within* the policy limits, a majority of the courts have held that this is definite evidence of bad faith. Some courts have held to the contrary, particularly where the contributions have been voluntary.

Magarick points out that the reasoning behind the decisions holding for the insurer seems to have been that such a contribution relieves, or could have relieved, the insured from the contingent liability for a possible excess verdict.[13] Magarick states, however, that this should not excuse an insurer whose unquestioned duty it is to protect its insured to the full extent of its policy limit.

A federal decision in New York declared that insurers:

> ... must tread the narrow and difficult line between merely informing the insured in a proper case of his chance to make a contribution (within the policy limits) in order to settle the case and insisting upon a contribution as a price of settlement ... insurers must be particularly careful not to do the latter or to use the possibility of contribution from the insured as a means of evading their own responsibilities.[14]

On the other hand, it has also been held that the *failure* by the insurer to solicit contribution to an offer of settlement *over* the policy limits was evidence of bad faith.[15]

Failure to Investigate Good faith requires diligent investigation of the facts of an accident. One might question whether the necessary elements of bad faith are present in the event of failure to *diligently* investigate. Is this failure "bad faith" conduct, as defined by the courts, or is it negligence?

Where the insurer fails to investigate the case properly, however, there is no question that the insurer is in breach of contract. Further, there is no question that the insurer has been negligent by omitting to conduct a proper investigation, one of the responsibilities under the contract. The right to recover for breach of contract or for the tort of negligence would seem to be apparent. Whether the failure to investigate constitutes an extraordinary showing of disingenuous or dishonest failure to carry out a contract is certainly a question of fact. It certainly demonstrates the existence of a nebulous threshold between negligence and what is considered to be "bad faith."

However, bad faith depends on the general attitude and conduct of an insurer, and insurers particularly get into trouble when they make a decision not to settle within policy limits, particularly if they have failed to make a diligent effort to thoroughly investigate the facts upon which an intelligent and good faith judgment may be predicated.[16] One insurer escaped liability for failure to adequately investigate a claim before rejecting demand for settlement only because the plaintiffs were unable to prove that they had been adversely affected by the violation.[17]

Rejection of Attorney's Advice Disregarding the advice of an insurer's independent legal counsel has served as a basis for bad faith recoveries. Insurers that refuse to follow the advice of their own counsel do so at their own peril.

In Chapter 1, it was pointed out that under the rules of discovery, the attorney-client privilege is not available in actions based on the alleged bad faith of the insurer. Consequently, if the claims file shows that the advice of the insurer's attorney was not followed, and an excess verdict results, the company can well be held responsible for bad faith conduct. It is important to note that not all courts are uniform on the matter of disregarding an attorney's advice.[18]

It is frequently the case in bad faith actions that insurers can successfully demonstrate good faith if they have followed the legal advice of counsel. This is important to remember in trying to avoid bad faith losses.

Failure to Inform Insured of Offer As clearly spelled out in the 1957 Brown case, the failure to inform the insured of an offer is a factor in a bad faith action. Timely communication with the insured is of utmost importance.

The insurer's fiduciary responsibility to protect the insured in a liability matter mandates that it keep the insured informed of all developments that could affect the interests of its insured during the life of a claim or a suit. Particularly important is the progress of any negotiations that might conclude the case.

Thus, the insurer has the duty to promptly advise its insured of any offers of settlement within the policy limits.

Failure to inform the insured of settlement offers has been held to be bad faith, although such failures have been held by a few courts to be an error in judgment. Given the modern development of bad faith law, however, it is difficult to agree with these latter decisions, either as a matter of law or in their assessment that an error in judgment excuses the insurer. The breach of fiduciary duty is quite apparent. The trend is to hold insurers responsible for a breach of fiduciary duty.

Where a third-party claimant has made an offer *which exceeds* the policy limits, courts have held that insurers are guilty of bad faith when they fail to notify the insured immediately of such offers. An insured is most interested in obtaining a settlement within the policy limits. Nevertheless, the circumstances of the claim and the gravity of the claimant's injuries may make it essential for the insured to be aware of offers in excess of policy limits, the reasoning being that the insured might consider contribution toward the full settlement amount.

Insured's Fault in Inducing Offer Rejection An insured's refusal to settle has relieved insurers of third-party bad faith liability in some cases. For example, some professional liability insurance policies require the insured's consent to any settlement. Some physician's malpractice liability policies and hospital liability policies still require that the insured's consent be secured before any settlement may be made. In one California case, for example, a hospital's liability insurance policy required it to pay a proportion of any damages paid to a claimant and required the hospital's consent to any settlement under the policy. The policy further provided a special arbitration procedure to resolve disagreements between the hospital and the insurer as to whether to settle a particular claim.

In this case the insurer's claims manager and attorney believed that the hospital was liable and recommended acceptance of the plaintiff's settlement demand. However, the hospital's administrator refused to settle. The matter proceeded to trial, and the plaintiff received a judgment in excess of her settlement demand. The plaintiff then sued the insurer, the hospital, and its administrators, alleging violation of California's Unfair Claims Practices Act.

The California Court of Appeal rejected the plaintiff's argument that the insurer's decision to accede to the hospital's wish not to settle rather than to compel arbitration raised a triable issue of fact as to third-party bad faith liability. Reasoning that the policy's arbitration provision was not intended for the plaintiff's benefit, the court held that she had no right to force it.[19]

Additional Factors Contributing to Bad Faith

Failure to Disclose Limits If the insurance limits are clearly inadequate to cover a claimant's loss, and if liability is reasonably clear, an insurer's concealment of the policy limits could well lead the claimant's attorney to believe that coverage is in excess of the offer. Such a concealment is a factor for jury determination of bad faith.[20] Where, for example, there is no question of liability and there is a serious injury, the insurer may have the duty to disclose the policy limits and offer the total amount in settlement. Where an excess verdict is likely, the insurer can protect itself from a bad faith action by disclosing the policy limits and attempting to protect the insured by offering the limits in full settlement.

Despite your natural inclination to save money on a settlement by not paying the full policy limits, remember that you must give as much consideration to the insured's interests as to those of the insurance company. To do otherwise subjects the insurer to a bad faith charge and possible liability in excess of policy limits. The disclosure of the policy limits is a definite factor in the claimant's evaluation of his or her claim and can be instrumental in influencing a possible settlement.[21]

If you prejudice the insured's interests by frustrating such settlement by trying to "save" money improperly, an excess judgment and a bad faith action against the insurer may be the logical consequence. In one case, the claims manager authorized the insurer's defense attorney to pay the full policy limits of $10,000. The attorney made some effort to "save" $500. An excess judgment against the insured was followed by a successful bad faith action by the insured. The court declared that the attorney violated his duty by acting "solely upon practical considerations in the interests of Allstate and considered his duties to the insurance company paramount to his duties to the insured."[22]

Where it seems inevitable that the claimant will recover in excess of the policy limits, it is foolhardy to conceal them and attempt to "economize" by offering less than the limits. The prudent course would seem to be to reveal the policy limits and offer them in total settlement in an attempt to protect the insured from an excess judgment. When such a course of "aggressive good faith" conduct is followed by the adjuster or defense counsel, it would be difficult following an excess judgment against an insured for that insured to prevail in a bad faith action.

Failure to Settle Within Policy Limits One thorny area of frequent litigation is the alleged bad faith failure of an insurer to settle a claim against its insured within the policy limits. The Brassil case clearly illustrated this perilous area of insurance claims handling.

It has been argued that in making a determination as to whether an insurer's failure to settle within policy limits amounts to bad faith, it must be shown that the claimant or his or her attorney have offered to settle within the policy limits. This is a prerequisite to liability of the insurer in the majority of cases. Where there is no indication that a case could have been settled within the policy limits, there should be no liability for an excess verdict.

However, this is not a universal rule, since courts have held insurers guilty of bad faith in spite of the fact that no offer of settlement had been made by the claimant within the policy limits. Where the claimant's injuries suggest that the policy limits will obviously be inadequate, one would not expect the claimant or his or her attorney to offer to settle within policy limits, even if the limits are known to the claimant and attorney. It would certainly be evidence of "aggressive good faith," however, if the insurer and defense counsel offered the total policy limits in an attempt to induce the claimant to settle for the policy limits. This would definitely be a good faith attempt to protect the best interests of the insured.

Inappropriate Economizing on Offers   In a 1974 New Jersey case, the insurance company had offered only part of a $50,000 policy, despite urgings by the insured's personal counsel. Claimant had not offered to settle within policy limits. The case, however, involved a plaintiff quadriplegic, and the likelihood of an excess judgment seemed to be apparent. The court repeatedly referred to the insurer as one in the role of fiduciary. In holding the insurer liable for the excess judgment, the court stated:

> ...since an insurer serves only its own interest by declining to compromise ... , a decision not to settle is perforce a selfish one. In attempting to save some of its own money on the policy, the company automatically exposes the insured to the risk of an excess judgment.[23]

Most adjusters are taught to be frugal with an insurer's money and to attempt to economize on claims settlements. Indeed, it is a natural course of action on the part of the adjuster to offer less than he or she believes a claim is worth, because the adjuster instinctively believes (and has good reason to believe) that a claimant will counter-claim with an amount in excess of the value of the loss.

Nevertheless, prudence dictates that offers, particularly "final" offers be realistically related to the gravity of the claimant's loss. Otherwise, insufficiency of the offer and the failure to offer the policy limits can well result in an excess verdict against the insured and subject an insurer to a bad faith action.

The Grievous Injury Cases   The Rova case discussed above, introduced the suggestion that in unusually serious claims, where it appears that the amount that will be awarded will unquestionably exceed policy limits, there is a duty upon the part of the insurer to offer the limits of the policy. The court stated that "where the carrier chooses not to offer limits of coverage, one wonders whether it should not bear the unhappy results of that unilateral decision."[24]

Courts have ruled that the failure to disclose policy limits deprives the claimant of the opportunity to evaluate his or her claim, and where the insurance company conceals policy limits, leading the claimant to believe that coverage was in excess of the offer, the jury is permitted to consider this factor in a bad faith determination. On the other hand, where the counsel for the claimant was offered the policy limits which he "could not reasonably have doubted" was the maximum coverage, the insurer was not liable for bad faith in not officially disclosing the exact amount of the policy limits.

The Rova case made it clear that there is a strong presumption of bad faith when an insurance company makes an offer that is grossly inadequate in light of the injury sustained by a plaintiff. Of course, the issue of whether there is liability is a pertinent consideration. If the insurance company in good faith contends that there is doubtful liability, it is certainly not unreasonable to permit the insurance company to attempt to disprove liability. However, where liability is clear, it is evidence of bad faith for an insurer to offer a grossly inadequate amount in settlement where the nature of the injury is so severe as to warrant the insurer offering the entire policy limits.

The idea that an insurance company had the duty to disclose its liability limits was a preposterous concept thirty years ago. Limits were kept absolutely confidential, and plaintiffs' attorneys went to great lengths attempting to discover the amount of that coverage, even going so far in some cases as to hire private investigators to ferret out the information.

Even in those days, however, competent insurance defense counsel might occasionally reveal policy limits in cases where coverage was grossly inadequate, and it was apparent that the entire policy limits would be exhausted in paying the claim. This was done in an honest attempt to protect the insured from an excess verdict.

Further, in such cases, since the insured is liable to end up paying part of the judgment, it is not unlikely that the insured may wish to take an active role in deciding whether a claim should or should not be settled. Thus a conflict of interest may occur which necessitates immediate communication with the insured. Failure to communicate with insureds advising them of their vulnerability to an excess judgment subjects the insurance company to possible bad faith situations, a point mentioned in the 1957 Brown case.

Rejection of Reasonable Offer If the insurance company rejects a reasonable offer within the policy limits, courts have held that the insurer's conduct is a manifestation of bad faith.[25] The Rova case has made it clear that it is definitely bad faith conduct for an insurer to make an *unreasonable* offer.

Unfortunately, claims adjusters, claims examiners, and attorneys are not infallible in their determination of what constitutes a reasonable valuation of a given injury. This is why it is so important that you conduct a thorough investigation, applying all pertinent financial information, medical records, and medical opinions regarding the prognosis on a personal injury claimant. Your fiduciary responsibility to the insured is to acquaint yourself thoroughly with all of the monetary aspects of the case and then work as hard as possible to keep the insured out of trouble, avoiding an excess judgment, if at all possible.

Combined with your duty to make a thorough investigation of all of the pertinent facts of a case, is the necessity for you to acquire experience and knowledge regarding what similar personal injury cases are worth. There are various services that are available to inform you of amounts that are typically awarded by juries in like cases.

Failure to Keep Insured Informed—In General We have already discussed the adjuster's duty to inform the insured of all offers. In addition, all developments that might affect the interest of an insured concerning the handling of the claim or the conduct of a lawsuit should be communicated immediately to an insured. In particular, courts have held that there is a responsibility to promptly advise the insured where there is a possibility of an excess judgment.

It is a routine, yet critical, claims handling procedure that a demand in excess of policy limits be communicated to the insured immediately by sending an "excess ad damnum" letter. The letter advises the insured that a demand has been made in excess of the policy limits and if the eventual judgment exceeds those, the insured will be personally liable to make up the balance.

The letter may also inform the insured that the company will appoint an attorney to defend any lawsuit that ensues. However, the insured may hire (and pay for) a personal attorney to collaborate with the insurer's counsel.

Most insurance claims departments write an "excess ad damnum" letter whenever there is any question about the loss potential of a claim. If the policy limits do not cover the entire amount of the judgment, the insured is responsible for the deficiency. Thus, it is highly important to advise the insured as soon as possible so that he or she has the option to obtain private counsel to represent him or her for any deficiency.

In the course of defending the insured in court, juries tend to look at defense counsel as representative of insurance companies. Any mistakes or conduct of such counsel are fertile areas for finding bad faith in any subsequent bad faith trial of the insurer. Where, on the other hand, a jury at the bad faith trial is made aware that the insured was advised in the beginning that he or she could secure a personal attorney, this could be considered evidence that the insurer acted in good faith to advise the insured of the prerogative to secure independent counsel.

There are other circumstances where the insurer is obligated to inform its insured. The investigation or the conduct of the trial may take an unfavorable turn, suggesting that an insured is about to lose the case or that the amount that will be recovered will exceed the policy limits. Quite obviously, the insured should be immediately notified of such developments.

Arbitrary or Capricious Conduct of Insurer Donaldson's definition of bad faith cited early in the chapter suggests conduct that is something other than negligence. Bad faith involves such things as dishonesty, fraud, concealment, and other improper behavior. The concept of bad faith, however, has been extended to include conduct that is not necessarily dishonest, but involves something more than mere "neglect."

Insurance company or adjuster conduct or claims settlement policy that tends to be arbitrary, inflexible, or capricious, violates the fiduciary responsibility of the insurer and its duty of good faith and fair dealing with the insured. The arbitrary or capricious handling of an insurance claim certainly shows disloyalty and unfair conduct not in keeping with the insured's interests.

The bad faith cases tend to place more emphasis upon the fiduciary responsibility and the special obligation that an insurance company and its claims personnel must treat the insured's interest with the same concern as that of the insurer's interest. It is for this reason that claims adjusters must be professional in their work, not permitting the burdens of case overloads, personal dislike or impatience with insureds or the rest of the public to influence their conduct. An emotional outbreak, imprudent language or conduct would be offensive to a jury when considering whether one has acted in good faith. It would certainly be germane to the jury's determination of whether the adjuster has acted in an arbitrary or capricious manner and to the detriment of the insured.

One knowledgeable author offers some excellent illustrations from actual claims files which could indicate arbitrary, capricious, indifferent, or irresponsible conduct by an insurer and its claims personnel:

> Our insured is insolvent. They can't collect a dime from him, so we'll take a chance on a jury verdict.

> We can settle within the policy limits, but maybe we can get the insured to kick in a couple thousand of dollars.

> Our insured's personal attorney is a probate lawyer and doesn't know what it's all about. We can just ignore him.

The plaintiff is a Negro (Jew, Italian, or whatever), and juries around here won't give him very much.

We never offer our policy limits.

Claimant's attorney gave us two weeks to accept his offer. The hell with him. Let's take our time.[26]

Clearly, comments such as these are improper whether they are expressed in words or in writing and may prove highly embarrassing for both the adjuster and the insurer when introduced into evidence in the course of a bad faith trial.

Other Factors   Virtually any sort of conduct on the part of the insurer that shows an absence of good faith can form the basis for a bad faith claim being brought against the insurer. Thus, there are many other factors, in addition to those that have been discussed previously, that can form the basis for a bad faith action.

A booklet published by the Insurance Committee for Arson Control gives examples of situations that may give rise to bad faith actions.[27] Of particular interest is the fact that a bad faith action may arise out of conduct of an insurer even prior to a loss. *Prior to loss* situations can include the following:

- False or misleading advertisement.
- False or misleading statements by the agent when explaining coverages, conditions, and exclusions.
- Failure to respond to inquiries by the insured or providing explanations when requested. Obviously, this may well be deemed a violation of the covenant of good faith at any stage of the insurance history.

The Committee includes these situations *following the loss* that may give rise to a bad faith claim:

- Failure to act upon notice of loss in a timely manner.
- Failure to investigate the loss in question in a timely and thorough manner.
- Undue and unexplained delays during any stage of the claims handling.
- Any conduct, practice, or procedures that appear to violate the principles of the Unfair Claims Practices Regulation, State Privacy Protection Act, etc.
- A failure to notify the insured or his attorney of the denial of the claim in a timely and straightforward manner and to set forth the reasons for the denial.

- Any harassment of the insured or his family and/or any defamatory comments in any stage of the proceedings may be used to show bad faith or, most certainly, lack of good faith.

The Committee's listing of factors that might lead to a bad faith action obviously includes some previously discussed in this chapter.

BAD FAITH ACTIONS AGAINST ADJUSTERS

Chapter 1 spelled out the dangers that confront the adjuster because of recent developments in the law regarding joint and several liability. The elimination or major revision of the joint and several liability rule subjects the employee acting on behalf of his or her employer to a major liability exposure.

In those states that have eliminated or modified their joint and several liability rule, fault will now be apportioned to joint tortfeasors, those parties responsible for damages sustained by a third party. The purpose of this new legislation, as indicated in Chapter 1, is to eliminate the "deep pockets" phenomenon.

Because of the changes occurring in the law, one can anticipate that there will be more claims and litigation brought directly against adjusters. Indeed, recent bad faith claims have been brought against independent insurance adjusters and their employees and against the employees of insurance companies.

At least four cases were brought in the state of California in 1986 against insurance adjusters.[28] In these four decisions, the California Courts of Appeal held that an independent insurance adjuster and its employees may be liable to insureds and third-party claimants for violations of the California Unfair Claims Practices Act, but that employees of insurance companies may not.

The critical inquiry in the cases appears to turn upon the interpretation of the statute in question. This leaves the question open whether adjusters can be held personally liable in bad faith claims in other jurisdictions.

A 1986 New Hampshire case held that an insured may bring a negligence action against an investigator hired by an insurer to investigate a claim.[29] Almost all courts that have addressed the issue of agents' or employees' liability for their company's bad faith have held that such agents and employees are not subject to liability for common law bad faith. These courts have reasoned that persons who are not parties to the insurance contract are not bound by the covenant of good faith and fair dealing.

Nevertheless, this is an area that is becoming dangerous for adjusters. Analysis of the liability of an insurance company's agent or employee (including the adjuster) should not stop with the covenant of good faith and fair dealing in contract law. Courts have permitted recovery from an insurer's attorneys, employees, adjusters, investigators, and agents on a variety of theories other than common law bad faith.

Thus, an insurance adjuster may be personally held liable for fraud, intentional infliction of emotional distress, invasion of privacy, breach of statutory duties, or under other theories of liability. This is another compelling reason why adjusters must practice "aggressive good faith" in the handling of all insurance claims if they wish to survive in the claims handling profession.

COMPARATIVE BAD FAITH

Recently, an interesting new legal defense has emerged from the bad faith litigation. This is the affirmative defense of comparative bad faith. Some cases have held that if an insured brings a bad faith action against the insurer, the insurer may raise the bad faith of the *insured* as an affirmative defense, either nullifying the claim of the insured or helping to mitigate the damages that the insurer subsequently must pay.

A late 1985 California case apparently is the first decision to recognize the affirmative defense of comparative bad faith.[30] In this case, the appellate court ordered the trial court to allow an insurer to utilize comparative bad faith to counter the insured's bad faith allegations.

The plaintiff suffered a loss compensable under the uninsured motorist provisions of her insurance policy. When her insurer refused to pay, the plaintiff submitted the claim for arbitration. The arbitrator decided for plaintiff, who then sued her insurer for bad faith.

The insurer answered, alleging the affirmative defense of bad faith conduct of the plaintiff and her attorney, and requested that any damages awarded plaintiff be reduced by the plaintiff's comparative bad faith. The appellate court could find no sound reason why the doctrine of comparative negligence should not be applicable in this situation.

The court reasoned that although the covenant of good faith and fair dealing arises out of a contractual relationship, breach of the duty is governed by tort principles. Thus, the court concluded:

> An insured's breach of the implied duty of good faith and fair dealing which contributes to an insurer's failure to pursue or delay in pursuing the investigation and payment of a claim may constitute at least a partial defense to plaintiff's damage action for the insurer's breach of its duty of good faith and fair dealing based on such delay or failure and, to the extent they may be the same, the insurer's or

agent's breach of their statutory duties under the unfair practices act.

In 1984, a California court had shown *some* willingness to accept the doctrine of comparative bad faith.[31] In this case, the parties agreed to submit a special verdict form to the jury providing for comparison of the bad faith conduct of the insured and insurer. The jury attributed 26 percent of the insured's general damages to her own bad faith conduct and reduced her damage award accordingly. The appellate court affirmed the trial court result, but refused to decide the propriety of the doctrine of comparative bad faith.

Since the special verdict form was submitted to the jury without objection, the issue of comparative bad faith was not raised on appeal in the 1984 case. However, the previously cited 1985 appellate court decision decided the issue when the court ruled that the affirmative defense of comparative bad faith is entirely appropriate.

It is quite possible that other jurisdictions will follow suit. Comparative negligence is widely recognized in tort law throughout the United States, and it is the logical extension of comparative negligence to recognize comparative bad faith. Further, California is a legal bellwether state, and other jurisdictions tend to follow new legal concepts introduced in the California courts.

COMMON BAD FAITH CASES

There are a number of claims areas that are most likely to result in bad faith cases brought against insurers.[32] The most common problem areas are discussed in the following sections.

Unfair Claims Practices

The enactment of Unfair Claims Settlement Practices statutes by most states has naturally led to a codification of conduct that is considered to be unfair. Obviously, it is a fertile area for substantiation of bad faith cases. Delay, procrastination, inadequate investigations, and a host of other situations result in bad faith claims. Unfortunate claims manual language and adjuster error and inexperience can make an insurer look bad to the jury.

Refusal to Defend

Where an insurer has reason to believe that there is no coverage, insurers have been under extreme stress trying to decide whether to defend the insured. Traditionally, the approach followed by insurers was to undertake a defense only if an insured signed a "non-waiver agreement" or after the insurance company has otherwise reserved its right to deny coverage.

The non-waiver agreement specifies that neither the insurer nor the insured waives any legal rights by the insurer's undertaking an investigation and subsequent defense of a claim. If subsequently it is determined that it had no liability toward the insured, it may legally withdraw from the defense of the insured without having waived its right to do so by undertaking a preliminary defense.

However, in 1984, in a California case, the court held that in a reservation of rights defense the company does not have the right to appoint defense counsel.[33] It is hard for an insurer to conduct a proper defense without having the right to appoint counsel. The reasoning of this case was repudiated by the Supreme Court of Washington in a 1986 decision that also reversed a Washington court of appeals decision which held that an insurer could be liable for failure to settle even where there was no coverage.[34]

The reservation of rights technique has long been a valuable tool for both insurer and insured, giving the insured necessary legal protection until the contract liability is determined. On the other hand, of course, one could argue that the insurer's right to select defense counsel places the attorney in a conflict of interest situation in which the attorney is being paid by the insurer but is representing the insured. It is most likely that we have not yet heard the last word regarding these reservation of rights matters.

Meanwhile, if there is any question whatsoever regarding contract liability, it is prudent for an insurer to consider undertaking the defense of an insured, with a reservation of rights, if appropriate, in order to avoid what could be a multi-million dollar award for bad faith.

Arson and Burglary Claims

Arson and burglary claims may present some difficult decisions for insurers and their claims personnel. It is obviously in the best interest of everyone concerned to immediately pay all just and proper claims. However, in the case of burglary and fire insurance claims, there is always the potential for fraud or arson committed by the insured.

Experienced claims personnel sometimes claim that they can actually "smell" a fraud or arson case. However, while circumstantial evidence can point to fraud or arson, a failure to dig deeper and evaluate a case from a juror's perspective can often result in a large bad faith verdict.

An objective, thorough investigation is the best defense in these cases. Healthy skepticism and suspicion is useful in the claims handling profession; however, one must not lose objectivity in these investigations. Jeffrey H. Leo, a Los Angeles attorney, describes a case won by his law firm in which an insured retail clothing store claimed that $100,000 worth of jeans had been stolen.

The police were skeptical because the retailer was behind on payments to his largest supplier, his books were inadequate as a proof of loss, and coverage had been purchased only two months prior to the incident. The insurer cross-complained against the plaintiff, claiming that the burglary was staged. A defense verdict was rendered on the insured's complaint, and $74,586 was awarded on the cross-complaint in favor of the insurer, for expenses, damages, and attorney's fees.

Failure to Pay Disability Benefits

Disability insurance policies were traditionally a fertile ground for "bad faith" lawsuits, but they are becoming less prevalent. The most important factor in avoiding these types of bad faith claims is to obtain exhaustive and reliable medical evidence to justify any denial of benefits. Both group and individual disability policy claims may be denied either because a disability is evaluated as non-permanent or as a result of a pre-existing condition.

Pre-Existing Conditions

Medical claims involving pre-existing illness naturally incite jurors' sympathy for someone who is ill or injured, and insurers frequently do not fair well in defending bad faith actions where they have denied claims arising out of pre-existing illnesses.

Once again the best defense on these cases is to secure exhaustive, reliable medical evidence as a justification for denial of benefits for pre-existing conditions. In all such matters, the insurer must maintain reasonable conduct in the handling of the claims. It is encouraging to note that high jury verdicts that are awarded in many of these cases are often substantially reduced on appeal.

Landslide and Flood Coverage Disputes

Landslide and flood coverage disputes have created an area of controversy where insurers have been sued for bad faith and punitive damages. This is particularly true in California. Illustrative of the problem were numerous landslide and flood claims brought against insurers following heavy rainfall in Southern California during 1980. Insurers denied coverage, arguing that the losses fell under flood or surface water exclusions. Plaintiffs, however, claimed that the damage had resulted from the acts or omissions of third parties—public agencies that had constructed inadequate storm control channels.

These were cases of "concurrent causation," where even though flood and surface water losses were not covered, plaintiffs argued that a concurrent cause—negligence of public agencies—*was* covered. When insurers denied coverage, they were sued for bad faith and punitive damages. In a major flood coverage case, *Safeco v. Guyton,* the California Ninth Circuit Court of Appeals threw out the bad faith and punitive damages claims and established a precedent for insurers to test genuine coverage issues without the specter of bad faith claims hanging over insurers.

Ascertaining the cause—or concurrent causes—of a loss is important in any case in order to avoid a bad faith case arising out of a coverage controversy. Needless to say, the possibility of multiple causes or concurrent causation is one that must be considered by adjusters. The problem and its solution is described in detail in the following sections.

THE SEPARATION OF ISSUES

The California landslide and flood case just described illustrates a particularly difficult problem for insurers and adjusters. Failure to pay claims based on honest reservations regarding questions of coverage can, nevertheless, subject insurers to potential bad faith liability.

That is why it is extremely important for adjusters to be alert to coverage controversies before denying claims. These cases require the closest scrutiny and evaluation.

Declaratory Judgments

If there is any question at all regarding a policy coverage case—any doubts whatsoever—before denial of the claim, the coverage question should be resolved. One writer comments:

> If a dispute appears to arise between an insured and insurer over a legitimate coverage issue, what is to prevent the insurer in good faith from seeking a declaratory judgment on the issue? The courts will not be likely to say there was bad faith, if the insurer honestly advises the insured that while they don't think there is coverage, they are willing to submit the matter to the court for the court's guidance. It is simply amazing how seldom insurers utilize this pathway to good faith![35]

Securing a declaratory judgment on coverage questions before deciding whether to pay a claim appears to be a prudent course of action. In difficult cases, where the insurer is faced with a complex coverage issue and a bad faith claim, it is desirable to try to resolve the coverage issue without being subject to liability for coverage, defense, or to bad faith claims. Jeffrey H. Leo reports success in the California case of *Safeco v. Guyton*. This case, he reports, has been relied upon by recent California decisions as authority for an insurer's right to test genuine coverage issues without the spectre of bad faith claims hanging over the head of the insurer and the claims manager or adjuster who mistakenly denies a claim that should have been paid.

Unfortunately, not all jurisdictions permit the separation of issues which permits the parties to resolve the coverage question before the insurer decides whether to pay a claim. In a recent decision, the Montana Supreme Court refused to permit separation of issues, declaring, "The policy of the law is to avoid multifariousness in litigation and to resolve all issues and lawsuits in one trial."[36]

BAD FAITH AND NEGLIGENCE

The preceding discussion has focused on the idea that bad faith has something to do with willful misconduct, dishonesty, fraud, duplicity, and so forth. Nevertheless, it is more and more apparent that it is a gross oversimplification and counterproductive to believe that bad faith depends entirely on the showing of evil intent.

Negligence

Negligence is conduct falling below the standard established by law for the protection of others against unreasonable risk of harm. The elements necessary to a cause of action based on negligence are:

1. A legal duty to conform to a standard of conduct for the protection of others against unreasonable risks.
2. A failure to conform to the standard.
3. A reasonably close causal connection between the conduct and the resulting injury.
4. Actual loss or damage resulting to the interests of another.[37]

Nowhere in the definition is there reference to willful misconduct, dishonesty, fraud, duplicity, disloyalty, or deceitful conduct. "Negligence is conduct, and not a state of mind."[38]

Yet the early cases cited in the first part of this chapter and Donaldson's definition of "bad faith" refer to "a state of mind," "a furtive design," or "some motive of ill will." Clearly, there is considerable lack of clarity in what constitutes bad faith. However, one thing that is abundantly clear is that courts and juries are tending to award bad faith damages in simple cases of negligence.[39]

One prominent insurance defense attorney states:

> In many cases and situations the distinctions between good faith or bad faith and negligence are really meaningless. The two theories for imposition of liability have coalesced in many cases, and further in many cases negligent acts on the part of an insurer have been used as the evidence to support a finding of the court that the insurer acted in "bad faith." Further, many courts have piggy-backed the two concepts and stated that an insurance underwriter must exercise good faith and due care in the negotiation and settlement of claims on behalf of its insured.[40]

For example, in one 1970 Oregon case, the court specifically found an insurer to have acted in good faith, but imposed excess liability because the insurer simply did not respond to a settlement demand within seven days due to "ordinary negligence." The court commented that "the fault arose out of bureaucratic bungling and assembly-line inefficiency, not bad faith."[41] Thus, excess liability can obviously arise from facts other than those indicating bad faith.

Negligence and You

If excess liability in a bad faith case can be imposed based upon fault consisting simply of "bureaucratic bungling and assembly-line inefficiency," this is clearly a standard of negligence. You can be held liable in bad faith actions for heedlessness or carelessness. The standard of negligence imposed by society is not necessarily based upon any moral fault of the individual. You can be held liable for stupidity, forgetfulness, an excitable temperament, or even sheer ignorance.

You should not be surprised, however, that bad faith claims can arise simply from negligence. If you read the provisions of the NAIC Model Unfair Claims Settlement Act that appear in Chapter 4, you will note that several of the unfair claims practices relate to a *failure* to act in a reasonable manner.

In addition, a large number of bad faith cases are decided against insurers because of "failure" to act in a fair, reasonable manner. Failure to act or an omission to act in a reasonable manner is negligence. It can also be the basis for bad faith actions—and sloppy, inefficient, careless, forgetful, negligent handling of claims can land an adjuster in court.

Chapter Notes

1. Liberty Mutual Insurance Company v. Altfillisch Construction Co., 70 C.A. 3rd 789 (1977).
2. There are exceptions to this rule. Some physicians' malpractice policies and hospital liability policies require the insured's consent to any settlement. The insurer's refusal to settle where the insured refuses to give consent does not subject the insurer to bad faith liability. See Carlile v. Farmers Exchange, 219 Cal. Rptr. 773 (1985).
3. James H. Donaldson, *Casualty Claim Practice*, 4th Ed. (Homewood, Illinois: Richard D. Irwin, 1984), pp. 973-974.
4. Weber v. Biddle, 483 P.2d 155 (Wash. 1971).
5. Gordon v. Nationwide Mutual Insurance Co., 285 N.E.2d 849 (N.Y. 1972).
6. Georgia Casualty Co. v. Mann, 46 S.W. 2d 777, 779 (Ky. 1932).
7. 210 N.Y. 235.
8. Henry G. Miller, "Living With Bad Faith," *Insurance Counsel Journal* (January 1979), p. 34.
9. Auerbach v. Maryland Casualty Co., 236 N.Y. 247 (1923).
10. Brown v. Guarantee Insurance Co., 319 P.2d 69 (Cal. 1957); see Miller, p. 34.
11. See Alan G. Buckner, "An Examination of 'Bad Faith' Tort" (Part One), *The National Underwriter* (December 10, 1982), p. 27, referring to Gruenberg v. Aetna Ins. Co., 108 Cal. Rptr. 480 (1973).
12. Brown v. Guarantee Insurance Co., p. 77.
13. Pat Magarick, *Excess Liability*, 2nd Ed. (New York: Clark Boardman Co., Ltd., 1982), p. 194-195.
14. Brochstein v. Nationwide Mutual Insurance Co., 448 F.2d 987 (2d Cir. N.Y. 1971).
15. Young v. American Casualty Co., 416 F.2d 906 (2d Cir. N.Y. 1967).
16. Weber v. Biddle.
17. Van Dyke v. St. Paul Fire and Marine Insurance Co., 448 N.E.2d 357 (Mass. 1983).
18. Olson v. Union Fire Ins. Co., 118 N.W. 2d 318 (Neb. 1960).
19. See Chapter Note 2.
20. Coppage v. Fireman's Fund Ins. Co., 379 F.2d 621 (6th Cir. Tenn. 1967).
21. Riske v. Truck Insurance Exchange, 490 F. 2d 1079 (8th Cir. N.D. 1974).
22. Lysick v. Walcom, 258 CAL. App. 136 (1958).
23. Rova Farms Resort, Inc. v. Investors Insurance Company of America, 323 A.2d 495 at 508 (N.J. 1974).
24. Rova Farms Resort, Inc. v. Investors Insurance Company of America, p. 509.
25. Magarick, p. 187.
26. Magarick, pp. 200-201.
27. Insurance Committee for Arson Control, *Good Faith* (January 1986). The Committee's address is 1501 Woodfield Road, Schamburg, Illinois 60195.

28. Bodenhamer v. Superior Court, 178 Cal. App. 3rd 180, 223 Cal. Rptr. 486 (Cal. App. 1986); Davis v. Continental Insurance Co., 178 Cal. App. 3rd 836, 224 Cal. Rptr. 66 (Cal. App. 1986); Grief v. Superior Court, 178 Cal. App. 3rd 984, 224 Cal. Rptr. 82 (Cal. App. 1986); Nelson v. GAB Business Services, Inc., 224 Cal. Rptr. 595 (Cal. App. 1986).
29. Morvay v. Hanover Ins. Co., 506 A.2d 333 (N.H. 1986).
30. California Casualty General Ins. Co. v. Superior Court   (Cal. App. 1985).
31. Fleming v. Safeco Ins. Co., 160 Cal. App. 3rd 31 (Cal. App. 1984).
32. Jeffrey H. Leo, *Perspectives* (Los Angeles, California: Parkinson, Wolf, Lazar, and Leo, Attorneys at Law, June 1986).
33. San Diego Navy Federal Credit Union v. Cumis Insurance Society, Inc., 162 Cal. App. 3rd 358, 208 Cal. Rptr. 494 (1984).
34. Tank v. State Farm Fire and Casualty Co., 105 Wash. 2nd 381, 715 P.2d 1133 (1986).
35. "The Bad-Faith Bears," *Insurance Adjuster* (December, 1982), p. 38.
36. Docket No. 84-322.
37. William L. Prosser, *Handbook of the Law of Torts* 4th Ed. (St. Paul, Minn.: West Publishing Company, 1971), p. 143.
38. Terry, Negligence, 1915, 29 Harv. L. Rev. 40.
39. Magarick, p. 221-222.
40. John H. Holmes, "Excess Liability for Bad Faith, or Is There More to It?" *The Independent Adjuster* (Summer, 1984), pp. 8-9.
41. Robertson v. Hartford, 333 F.Supp. 739 (D.C. Ore. 1970).

CHAPTER 3

Punitive Damages

The concept of punitive damages is one that has undergone considerable discussion over the last century. Considerable controversy rages even today regarding what situation should give rise to punitive damages.

The traditional concept of punitive damages was spelled out in the classic 1941 book on torts authored by William L. Prosser. In that book he likened the concept of punitive damages to a punishment that was rendered by the courts in those tort situations that were frequently associated with crime. He explained that there must be something more serious than a mere ordinary tort. There must be circumstances of aggravation or outrage, or a conscious and deliberate disregard of the interests of others so that the conduct of the individual could be called willful or wanton. Prosser expressed the traditional concept of punitive damages as follows:

> ...the ideas underlying the criminal law have invaded the field of torts. Where the defendant's wrongdoing has been intentional and deliberate, and has the character of outrage frequently associated with crime, all but a few courts have permitted the jury to award in the tort action "punitive" or "exemplary" damages, or what is sometimes called "smart money." Such damages are given to the plaintiff over and above the full compensation for his injuries, for the purpose of punishing the defendant, of teaching him not to do it again, and of deterring others from following his example. Something more than the mere commission of a tort is always required for punitive damages: there must be circumstances of aggravation or outrage, such as ill will or a fraudulent or evil motive on the part of the defendant, or such a conscious and deliberate disregard of the interests of others that his conduct may be called willful or wanton.[1]

BAD FAITH AND PUNITIVE DAMAGES

In the preceding chapter on the subject of bad faith, we explored the circumstances under which courts and juries would award extra-contractual damages to parties injured by the bad faith conduct of insurers. We noted that there has been an evolution in the development of bad faith law from the concept of a breach of contract or a breach of the implied warranty of good faith. From a simple breach of contract, the courts have expanded the concept of bad faith to a tort.

The tort ordinarily contemplated in a bad faith action involved actual or constructive fraud, or design to mislead or deceive another or a refusal to fulfill some duty or some contractual obligation. Bad faith was considered to be prompted by sinister motive, contemplating a state of mind that operated within a furtive design or some motive of interest or ill will.

In other words, bad faith contemplated action over and above honest mistakes of judgment or conduct that would ordinarily be categorized as negligence—failure to act in a reasonable manner. We have noted, however, that the tort of bad faith has been extended by some courts to include the tort of negligence, so that the dividing line between the traditional concept of bad faith and that of negligence sometimes becomes indistinguishable.

Nevertheless, it was the element of outrageous, fraudulent, malicious, or oppressive behavior that established the strong connection between bad faith law and the awarding of punitive damages. One cannot discuss the subject of punitive damages without discussing their relationship to bad faith torts.

In this discussion we must distinguish between jurisdictions that consider bad faith as merely a breach of contract, that is, a breach of the implied covenant of good faith and those jurisdictions that consider bad faith as a tort.

If it is the law in a specific jurisdiction that in a bad faith case we are dealing only with a breach of contract situation, then damages for emotional distress and punitive damages are not recoverable. In Kansas, for example, damages for breach of contract are limited to pecuniary losses sustained. Exemplary or punitive damages are not recoverable in the absence of an independent tort.[2]

> This exception to the rule of unavailability of punitive damages in breach of contract actions is recognized when some independent tort or wrong results in additional injury which justifies the assessment of punitive damages by way of punishment of the wrongdoer. In such a case the proof of the independent tort must indicate the presence of malice, fraud or wanton disregard for the rights of others.[3]

However, if the jurisdiction determines bad faith *is* a tort, damages for emotional distress and also punitive damages might be recoverable if the essential elements of fraud, malice, or oppression are present. In those jurisdictions that recognize bad faith as a tort, there must be "the character of outrage frequently associated with crime." Yet courts today have also ruled that punitive damages naturally flow from the tort of bad faith breach of contracts.[4]

The foregoing discussion is primarily a theoretical one. Prosser's forty-five year old commentary regarding punitive damages spelled out the prevailing law forty-five years ago, at least for the state courts. Today, however, some courts are tending to become more liberal in what constitutes conduct that justifies the imposition of punitive damages by courts and juries. To understand the changes that have occurred, a historical discussion is in order.

EARLY HISTORY OF PUNITIVE DAMAGES

The nature of punitive or exemplary damages has long been associated with conduct that appears to be almost criminal in nature. Thus, it has been a policy to provide for some punishment of the offender, short of charging the offender with a crime. This has been accomplished by the awarding of punitive damages.

A criminal offense is one against the public at large, for which the state, as the representative of the public, will bring proceedings in the form of a criminal prosecution. The intent of the prosecution, of course, is to punish the offender or remove him or her from society, while at the same time deterring others from imitating the offender.

The civil action for a tort, on the other hand, was designed initially to compensate an injured person for damage suffered. The offender is forced to pay a sum of money to recompense the injured person. Compensatory damages are awarded. The state's interest is not involved in these individual tort actions.

With the adoption of the concept of "punitive" or "exemplary" damages, the law introduced the concept of a non-criminal action which nevertheless punished the wrongdoer financially. It has long been the public policy to try to attempt to prevent future harm by using civil damages as a way to punish the wrongdoer. Thus, punitive damages have provided an incentive to deter individuals from conducting their affairs in a manner that will harm others.

Prevention is fortified by financial punishment of the offender for what he or she has already done, since the punishment will prevent repetition of the offense. Even in the case of compensatory damages (those damages that mainly compensate for actual dollars lost) there is a belief that what is paid to the plaintiff is taken away from the defendant, and this in and of itself affords some punishment or retribution. Compensatory damages, however, are usually treated by the judicial system as a mere adjustment of loss which has occurred and which justice dictates should be paid to the injured party. When we inject the aspect of punitive or exemplary damages, however, both prevention and retribution become accepted objects of the administration of the law of torts.

CRIMINAL ASPECT OF PUNITIVE DAMAGES

To grant punitive damages is to punish. It is punishment for conduct which is "almost" criminal in nature. But if we are dealing with quasi-criminal conduct and meting out punishment, it seems inconsistent with legal theory to punish a defendant without granting him or her the legal safeguards that criminal law affords an accused defendant in the criminal matter.

Defendant's Lack of Safeguards

In the early cases involving the granting of punitive damages for torts, there was much controversy. Granting punitive damages as a form of punishment seemed to be improper to many legal scholars, because the usual safeguards of criminal procedure were not available to the defendant where such damages are granted. The safeguards of criminal procedures require such things as proof of guilt beyond a reasonable doubt, the privilege against self-incrimination, and even the rule against double jeopardy, since the defendant may still be prosecuted for the crime after he has been mulcted in the tort action.[5]

There is another legal point that has been brought up by scholars regarding punitive damages. If the awarding of punitive damages is quasi-criminal in nature, that is, those damages are granted as a way to punish the defender and to deter others from engaging in similar conduct, there is a principle of criminal law that would suggest that any amount extracted from the defendant in the way of punishment should be paid to the state as is the case in criminal actions where a defendant is fined. Fines extracted in criminal cases go to the state. In the case of punitive damages awarded in a tort action, however, the damages go to the plaintiff in the tort action.

In criminal law, the criminal act impacts on society, and any fine extracted from the defendant goes to society. It follows then, that if punitive damages are awarded in a tort action because of what appears to be quasi-criminal behavior on the part of the defendant, any damages recovered against the defendant for the defendant's bad behavior should also go to society rather than to individual plaintiffs.

This line of reasoning is not irrelevant today. A number of writers today have suggested that one way to cut down on the amount of punitive damage awards by courts and verdicts by juries would be to grant punitive damages as an award to the State rather than to the individual claimants. The rationale for making such awards would follow the reasoning which is applied in the case of criminal fines: the defendant would be punished appropriately; and perhaps courts and juries would be less likely to make unreasonable awards for punitive damages if they knew the money was going to the State rather than to a private litigant. This reasoning has received some attention recently, since legislation providing for such disposition of punitive damages has been advocated by some legislators and legal scholars.

A Compensatory Aspect of Punitive Damages

On the other hand, it has been widely believed by some legal scholars that compensatory damages have not been an adequate remedy in some cases to provide compensation for an injured plaintiff. Punitive damages were encouraged as a partial remedy for the defect in American civil procedure which denied some compensatory damages. For example, plaintiffs certainly should be entitled to some compensation for actual expenses of litigation, such as counsel fees and as an incentive to bring into court and redress a long array of cases of outrage and oppression which in practice escaped the notice of prosecuting attorneys occupied with serious crime.

The U.S. Supreme Court has noted the compensatory aspect of punitive damages, observing that in some cases punitive damages are necessary to provide some redress. For example, in a 1980 decision the U.S. Supreme Court ruled that "punitive damages may be the only significant remedy available...where constitutional rights are maliciously violated but the victim cannot prove compensable injury.[6]

Motives and Conduct

The early courts, however, did not contemplate granting punitive damages for simple breaches of contract. Punitive or exemplary damages were awarded in cases of such outrageous or evil conduct that there always seemed to be the element of intent present. Typical of the torts for which punitive damages were awarded in earlier days were such torts as assault and battery, libel and slander, deceit, seduction, and intentional interferences with property, such as trespass or conversion. Even in the early days of the granting of punitive damages, however, it was not so much the particular tort committed as the defendant's motives and conduct in committing it.

This early theory is certainly applicable today and leaves the door open for the awarding of damages in unfair claims settlement practices. Juries have found it easy to detect outrageous, willful, and wanton conduct of defendant insurers and their claims personnel. Where the defendant's motives have been unusually suspect, it has been easy for juries to justify large verdicts awarding punitive damages.

A review of some of the fact situations arising out of bad faith claims fortifies the conviction that an insurer's motives fell within the type of deplorable conduct that warrants punitive damages. Prosser stated:

> In many questions of tort liability, the motive or purpose behind a defendant's conduct plays a predominant part. His liability then will usually depend upon the importance and social value attached to his objectives, balanced against the nature of the plaintiff's interests and the extent of the harm to them.[7]

Earlier common law took little or no account of the motives of the defendant. A bad motive, while it might aggravate compensatory damages, was considered of no significance unless a tort could not be made out without it. (The law followed by the Kansas courts today.) By the beginning of the eighteenth century, however, such a motive was first held to be sufficient in itself to determine liability.

Early tort law permitted a defendant to use all reasonable force to exclude others from his land or eject a trespasser to resort to legal process to collect a valid debt or to recover from a tortfeasor, or to refuse entirely to deal with one to whom he or she is not under contract, all in the worst possible spirit of malevolent vindictiveness. The defendant could still claim immunity from all liability. Modern law gives us a different picture.

MODERN LAW AND PUNITIVE DAMAGES

Modern law began to inquire into the character of a defendant's motives in his or her behavior. It was inevitable that the defendant's motives should be examined. Modern law has been extended to such lengths by statute and by court interpretation to include a responsibility of fair play toward persons with whom the defendant has no contractual relationship. We find this apparent when we examine the trend of the law to grant third-party claimants the right to a direct right of action against an insured's insurance company.

Under modern law, where the court determines that bad faith is a tort, damages for emotional distress and also punitive damages, as previously noted, may be recovered from the defendant if fraud, or malice or oppression is present. This is usually the ruling in most courts. There are other courts that award punitive damages in cases of gross negligence or intoxication.

Gross Negligence or Intoxication

There have been situations where courts have departed from the requirement of showing fraud, malice, or oppression in order to award punitive damages. A California court, for example, ruled that gross negligence or even intoxication is sufficient to uphold a punitive damages award.[8] This line of reasoning is discussed in an article written by Victor B. Levit, Chairman of the Professional Liability Committee of the American Bar Association. He writes:

> Just as the trend is ever upward in the size of punitive awards, the legal requirements to sustain any award of punitive damages are being lowered, thus making it easier to recover punitive damages.[9]

U.S. SUPREME COURT STANDARD FOR PUNITIVE DAMAGES

We tend to think of decisions of the United States Supreme Court as being the "law of the land." This is not necessarily true. In those cases where no federal issue is involved, or where a state law is not repugnant to the U.S. Constitution, the state law is applied and controls. In diversity of citizenship cases, as a matter of fact, federal judges apply the law of the state in which the case is being heard.

It is a little known fact to most Americans that until the administration of Chief Justice Earl Warren (1953-1969), some of the Bill of Rights of the U.S. Constitution were not practiced in state courts. For example, the Fifth Amendment, which grants you the right to refuse to incriminate yourself by having to take the witness stand and testify against yourself, was not binding upon state courts until the Warren Court applied that Constitutional right to the trial procedure of state courts.

Most of the cases that you will be most interested in will be those involving your own jurisdiction and the law of your own states in the area of bad faith law, punitive damages, and the unfair claims settlement practices statutes. Nevertheless, the decisions of the U.S. Supreme Court are highly important and tend to be quite persuasive in helping to establish state law in some situations. Consequently, we must be familiar with the interpretation of law rendered by the highest court of our land, even though it now may not coincide with our own state's laws. It is not unlikely that the Supreme Court decisions will influence future changes in our own state's laws.

In 1983 the Supreme Court established the definitive federal law relating to the subject of punitive damages. This was set forth in the case of *William H. Smith v. Daniel R. Wade.*

This case is particularly interesting because there are two diametrically opposed viewpoints regarding the subject of punitive damages. The majority barely prevailed in a five to four decision rendered by the Court. A long-time liberal associate justice of the Court, William J. Brennan, rendered the majority decision on behalf of the five-member majority.

The opposing viewpoint, or dissenting viewpoint, of the court was presented in a lengthy dissenting opinion written by then Associate Justice William Rehnquist, who became Chief Justice in 1986.

An examination of the majority opinion and the dissenting opinion in this case will help to explain the federal law relating to punitive damages. It will also provide an exposition of the evolution of state law on the subject.

The Majority Opinion

The majority of the court in *Smith v. Wade* upheld a punitive award granted in a civil rights suit against a prison guard, based on the "cruel and unusual" punishment provision of the Eighth Amendment to the United States Constitution. The Supreme Court effectively abandoned the requirements of fraud, malice, or oppression by declaring that most states allow punitive damages for something less than intentional conduct, such as gross negligence.[10]

The case was brought against a reformatory guard by an inmate. Confined to a Missouri reformatory, the youthful first offender complained that he was harassed, beaten, and sexually assaulted by his cellmates. He brought suit under 42 U.S.C. § 1983, alleging that his Eighth Amendment rights had been violated. Section 1983 was derived from the Civil Rights Act of 1871 which provided:

> Every person who, under color of any statute, ordinance, regulation, custom, or usage, of any State or Territory or the District of Columbia, subjects, or causes to be subjected, any citizen of the United States or other person within the jurisdiction thereof to the deprivation of any rights, privileges, or immunities secured by the Constitution and laws, shall be liable to the party injured in an action at law, suit in equity, or other proper proceedings for redress.

The inmate sought not only compensatory damages but punitive damages as well.

The majority of the Court concluded that at the time of the enactment of the 1871 Act, the availability of punitive damages was accepted as settled law by nearly all state and federal courts. The Court held that the common law both in 1871 and in 1983 allows for recovery of punitive damages in court cases not only for actual malicious intent, but also for reckless indifference to the rights of others.

The majority decision concedes that there was considerable debate about the theoretical correctness of the punitive damages doctrine in the latter part of the last century, but contends unequivocally that the doctrine was accepted as settled law by nearly all state and federal courts, including the U.S. Supreme Court.

Particularly pertinent is the observation of the Court that the law is dynamic—ever changing. The Court remarked that when the language of the particular statute and its legislative history provide no clear answer to a contemporary problem, today's Court will look at the present social climate and law.

The Court finds useful guidance in the law prevailing at the time when the Act was passed; but it does not follow that that law is absolutely controlling, or that current law is irrelevant. The Court remarked:

> On the contrary, if the prevailing view on some point of general tort law had changed substantially in the intervening century (which is not the case here), we might be highly reluctant to assume that Congress intended to perpetuate a now-obsolete doctrine.

There was considerable variation among American jurisdictions in the latter part of the nineteenth century on the precise standard to be applied in awarding punitive damages—a variation that was aggravated by trying to define such ambiguous common terms as "malice" and "gross negligence." Most of the confusion, however, seemed to arise over the degree of negligence, recklessness, carelessness, or culpable indifference that should be required—not whether actual intent was essential.

The Court then proceeds to discuss the meaning of "wantonness," "willfulness," and "malice." After defining the terms, the Court declared that the large majority of state and lower federal courts was in agreement that punitive damage awards did not require a showing of actual malicious intent. They permitted punitive awards on variously stated standards of negligence, recklessness, or other culpable conduct short of actual malicious intent.

The Court cited an 1869 Connecticut case in support of its conclusions and as an illustration of the thinking of state courts. In the case of Welch v. Durand[11] the Court ruled that punitive damages were proper where the defendant's pistol bullet, fired at a target, ricocheted and hit the plaintiff. The Court ruled that punitive damages were proper in cases of malicious or wanton misconduct or culpable neglect of the defendant. In this particular case, the defendant was guilty of wanton misconduct and culpable neglect. The Court ruled that it was immaterial that the injury was unintentional, and that punitive damages were warranted if an act was wanton, reckless, without due care, and grossly negligent.

No Express Right to Punitive Damages　One point that the majority of the Court stressed was the fact that a plaintiff is not entitled to punitive damages as a matter of right, no matter how bad the defendant's conduct. The question of whether to award punitive damages is always left to the determiner of fact, whether it be a judge or a jury. The trier of fact may or may not make an award of punitive damages. It is a discretionary matter.

This is in contrast to compensatory damages, which are mandatory. Once liability is found, a jury is required to award compensatory damages in an amount appropriate to compensate the plaintiff for the loss sustained. Punitive damages, on the other hand, are awarded in the jury's discretion "to punish the defendant for his outrageous conduct and to deter him and others like him from similar conduct in the future."

Proper instructions to the jury usually take the following form:

> If you find the issues in favor of the plaintiff, and if the conduct of one or more of the defendants is shown to be a reckless or callous disregard of, or indifference to, the rights or safety of others, then you *may* assess punitive or exemplary damages in addition to any award of actual damages. (Emphasis added)

Majority's Final Ruling　The majority of the Court affirmed the judgment of the lower court and held that a jury may be permitted to assess punitive damages when the defendant's conduct is shown to be motivated by evil motive or intent, *or* when it involves reckless or callous indifference to the federally protected rights of others. The Court held that this threshold applies even when the underlying standard of liability for compensatory damages is one of recklessness.

The Dissenting Opinion—Justice Rehnquist

Justice Rehnquist maintained in the dissenting opinion that the proper standard for an award of punitive damages requires at least some degree of improper motive on the part of the defendant. He argued that some sort of "evil intent"—and not mere recklessness—was necessary to justify an award of punitive damages.

In analyzing the case, Rehnquist examined the fundamental purpose of damages. He stated that damages are awarded to compensate the victim—to redress the injuries that the victim actually has suffered.

In contrast, the doctrine of punitive damages permits the award of damages far beyond the most generous conception of actual injury. This award of punitive damages is rationalized principally on three grounds: (1) punitive damages are assessed for the avowed purpose of punishing the defendant; (2) such damages will deter persons from violating the rights of others; and (3) such damages provide a "bounty" that encourages private lawsuits to assert legal rights. Justice Rehnquist's narrow conception of the purpose of punitive damages would go against the reasoning that there is a compensatory aspect of punitive damages, as brought out in the 1980 U.S. Supreme Court case of *Carlson v. Green.* Justice Rehnquist also brought up the quasi-criminal nature of punitive damages and the absence of the safeguards that are present in criminal proceedings to protect the rights of defendants. He deplores the fact that punitive damages are frequently based upon the caprice and prejudice of jurors and that they are employed to punish unpopular defendants, awarding damages in wholly unpredictable amounts bearing no particular relation to the actual harm caused. Justice Rehnquist then cited a number of American state jurisdictions that refuse to condone punitive damage awards and some that limit the amount of punitive damages that may be awarded.

Referring to a common dictionary to try and define the terms that are employed by some courts in the awarding of punitive damages, Mr. Rehnquist concluded that the law of punitive damages is characterized by a high degree of uncertainty that stems from the use of a multiplicity of vague, overlapping terms. He concluded that "malice" imports an actual ill will, intent, or improper motive requirement. The term "wanton," he suggested, requires an inquiry into the motive and intentions of the defendant. "Willfulness," in the Justice's opinion, indicates that there is design, purpose, and intent to do wrong and inflict injury.

Justice Rehnquist also cited the 1852 case of *Day v. Woodworth*, in which the Court made perfectly clear that punitive damages cannot be awarded, absent actual evil motive.[12] The Court further reasoned that punitive damages are predicated on the "malice, wantonness, oppression, or outrage of the defendant's conduct." The Court went further and stated that punitive damages are awarded because of "moral turpitude or atrocity." This standard certainly suggests criminal behavior.

Particularly persuasive is the argument that to use a standard that contemplates willful misconduct or an intentional act along with negligent behavior (even if it is gross negligence), presents a confusing standard. As a 1911 Missouri court remarked: "When willfulness enters, negligence steps out. The former is characterized by advertence, and the latter by inadvertence."[13]

Justice Rehnquist continued to attack the majority decision by observing that the legal treatises in use in the 1870s do not support the majority's assertion that punitive damages could be awarded on a showing of gross negligence, recklessness, or serious indifference to the rights of others. He also disagreed with the majority's conclusion that most jurisdictions followed the legal reasoning of the majority decision.

Observing that different states applied different rules, Justice Rehnquist stated that the decisions rendered by state courts in the years preceding and immediately following the 1871 Act attest to the fact that a solid majority of jurisdictions took the view that the standard for an award of punitive damages included a requirement of ill will. Ill will, he argued, contemplates something more than reckless or callous indifference to the rights of others.

In conclusion, Mr. Rehnquist argued that there is a "universal and persistent" linkage in our law between punishment and wrongful intent. Thus, it is anomalous, and counter to deeply-rooted legal principles and common-sense notions to punish persons who meant no harm, and award a windfall, in the form of punitive damages, to someone who already has been fully compensated. To expand the concept of punitive damages to a vaguely defined, elastic standard like "reckless indifference" gives free rein to the biases and prejudices of juries.

In Conclusion

Legislative intent of the legislators who enacted in 1871 statute is obviously pertinent in a court's enforcement and interpretation of that Act. However, in this case, little legislative intent was available for the court to evaluate. The 1983 judges of the U.S. Supreme Court, however, noted that many of the members of the 1871 U.S. Legislature were attorneys and would therefore be familiar with common law. In their interpretation of the 1871 statute, therefore, they turned to the court decisions as a way of attempting to ascertain legislative intent of the 1871 Congress.

Significance of Smith v. Wade The 1983 *Smith v. Wade* U.S. Supreme Court case is certainly instructive in giving us some insight into federal judicial thinking on the subject of punitive damages. Its significance, however, may not be particularly monumental for a number of reasons. As already observed, the composition of the court has changed so that it is a distinct possibility that the *Smith v. Wade* case may be reversed if a similar case comes before a more conservative composition of judges.

Aside from the foregoing consideration, although the decisions of the U.S. Supreme Court are persuasive and sometimes highly influential in state courts, nevertheless most of the law which claims adjusters and claims counsel must contend with today in the area of punitive damages is that law which has been set forth by the state courts.

It must also be remembered that the *Smith v. Wade* case turned on the interpretation of a statute, although common law was prominently discussed in the deliberations of the court. Most punitive damage cases, however, turn directly upon the court's interpretation of what the common law is in a particular state and do not always involve the court in trying to interpret the legislative intent of a state legislature when it enacted a state statute.

The significance is that the determination of legislative intent of the U.S. Congress when it enacted an 1871 statute may not be particularly pertinent in today's era of consumerism and judge and jury sympathy toward the plight of individual litigants. As noted previously in this book, the legal climate in the United States has changed tremendously during the last century to place more emphasis upon the right of consumers and to be more critical of the large, impersonal corporation.

We are all aware that insurance companies have not been particularly popular with the insuring public. Survey after survey in recent years has shown a pronounced displeasure with insurers' handling of insurance claims. Thus, this explains the rationale for the enactment of the unfair claims settlement practices statutes by virtually every state in the United States.

Smith v. Wade *Is Instructive* It is important to note the legal arguments that are advanced by the courts in connection with the subject of punitive damages. One must always be alert, however, that the more liberal interpretation of the right to punitive damages as articulated by the majority ruling of the *Smith v. Wade* case could well become a popular interpretation for expanding the rights of individual litigants in their suits against insurance companies.

The trend in the law of damages has been to provide greater remedies and more liberal remedies to insureds in their suits against insurers. The individual claims adjuster must be most mindful of the fact that conduct in the handling of insurance claims must avoid any and all of the grounds specified for the awarding of punitive damages articulated either by the majority of the U.S. Supreme Court or by the dissenting judges, as represented by Chief Justice Rehnquist.

PUNITIVE DAMAGES—ADEQUACY OR EXCESSIVENESS

As a general proposition, the courts have left the amount to be awarded in punitive or exemplary damages to the discretion of the trier of facts. This, of course, would be the judge, where there is no jury, or a jury, where the parties have requested one.

Courts have intervened in jury awards only in those instances where the award was deemed to be grossly excessive or the result of passion or prejudice on the part of the jury. Among the factors considered by the courts in determining whether an award is grossly excessive or the result of passion or prejudice are the relationship between the punitive and compensatory damages, the nature and consequences of, or intent involved in the act complained of, and the financial status or condition of the defendant. Also considered are such miscellaneous factors as the amount historically awarded in similar cases, the amount of criminal fine or penalty applicable for a similar act, and statutes which may limit the amount of punitive damages recoverable.

Need for Knowledge of Damage Standards

The huge jury verdicts which have been awarded for punitive damages in recent years suggest that adjusters, juries, and attorneys should become more familiar with the historical standards that have been applied in cases where verdicts have been either drastically reduced or else increased because of either excessiveness or inadequacy.

One excellent publication that provides a plethora of cases dealing with excessiveness and inadequacy of punitive damage awards is the *American Law Reports*. This is a legal publication that can be found in any good law library. It should be turned to as a valuable source in furnishing guidance to litigants, their attorneys, and the courts. This is particularly true especially as to the outer limits of an award, above or below which the amount awarded will probably be considered an abuse of discretion.

Elsewhere in this book reference is made to a case where a woman was granted $988,000 in a jury award when she claimed that she had lost her psychic power after receiving a dye in preparation for a CAT-scan at a hospital. The trial judge overturned the award, stating that the award was "grossly excessive and a shock to the court's sense of justice." The judge ordered a new trial. Although the print media does an over-zealous job of reporting huge jury verdicts, seldom does the reading public hear that on subsequent appeal those awards often have been drastically reduced.

Some juries have been so enthusiastic in their granting of punitive damages that they have actually awarded damages in excess of the amount that the plaintiff has requested in his or her complaint. In one 1980 Texas case, for example, the jury awarded $150,000 in punitive damages in a wrongful death action, even though the plaintiff had asked for only $100,000. The judge reduced the award to the amount asked for in the complaint, since the amount of punitive damages awarded could not exceed the amount demanded in the complaint. This was a case where the plaintiff's attorney apparently was unaware of the amount of punitive damages which had been upheld in similar cases within the jurisdiction. One element that a court always examines in an award of punitive damages is the ability of the defendant to pay the award. As an adjuster, you must always remember that a defendant's ability to pay and insurance coverage will influence a jury. This factor must be considered in your evaluation of a case.

Award Final in Absence of Passion or Prejudice There are a number of jurisdictions where the courts have adopted the view that the amount of punitive or exemplary damages awarded in an action involving personal injury or death must be left to the sound discretion of the trier of fact. Absent a showing of passion or prejudice, the award of the jury will not be set aside on grounds of excessiveness or inadequacy. An Alabama court in 1957, for example, ruled that an award of punitive damages should not be ruled excessive unless there was a showing that the jury made the award as a result of passion, prejudice, corruption, or mistake. The court ruled that the jury did not have an unbridled or arbitrary discretion to award damages, but if punitive damages were arrived at with "legal, sound and honest discretion," they should be left undisturbed.

Similarly, courts in California have ruled that the amount of punitive damages to be awarded must be left to the discretion of the jury, and courts should not interfere unless the amount awarded is so grossly excessive as to shock the moral sense and raise a reasonable presumption that the jury in the rendition of the verdict was actuated and influenced by passion or prejudice.

A Missouri court in 1937 determined that insofar as punitive damages are concerned, they are so purely and peculiarly a matter for the jury's discretion that regardless of what the character of the action may be, it is only in an extreme case that an appellate court will undertake to revise such an award. In a similar case in Pennsylvania in 1977, the court ruled that a judge should be extremely reluctant to interfere with the time-honored power of the jury in the exercise of its collective judgment to assess damages. Nevertheless, the court held that a punitive damage award may be set aside as excessive to the extent that the result is shocking, unfair, and biased. The jury's award must have been clearly influenced by partiality, passion, prejudice, or a misconception of the law as given to it by the judge before an award may be set aside.

Relationship to Compensatory Damages Some courts have used the amount of compensatory damages awarded as one factor to be considered when determining the propriety of the amount of a punitive damage award in actions involving personal injury or death. Punitive damage awards must bear some reasonable relationship to the amount of compensatory damages granted.

In a 1977 California case, for example, the court ruled that the punitive damage award would be found to be excessive as a matter of law where it was so grossly disproportionate to the amount of compensatory damages as to raise the presumption that it was a result of passion or prejudice. Although the court set no fixed ratio upon which to determine the priority of the punitive damage award, punitive damages should bear a reasonable relationship to the compensatory damages awarded, the court declared.

A 1981 Colorado court rejected the contention that there is some ratio that exists between compensatory damages and the amount of punitive damages awarded. The defendant contended that the ratio of actual damages to punitive damages should be no more than two to one. The court stated that there was no fixed mathematical ratio to determine the amount of an appropriate punitive damage award.

A 1970 Delaware court similarly held that there was no set rule or ratio between the amount of compensatory damages and punitive damages that could be established. Delaware courts had adopted the rule that an award of punitive damages must not be disproportionate compared to the award given for compensatory damages. However, a court concluded that the proportionality rule meant that viewing the circumstances and facts of the case, the degree of maliciousness, wantonness, or grossness shown by a defendant's conduct and the extent of injuries caused, judgment for punitive damages should not be so excessive as to indicate that the jury acted out of passion or prejudice rather than out of calmly-reasoned deliberation. Only if the amount of punitive damages when compared to the amount of compensatory damages awarded, in light of other factors, is grossly excessive as to shock the judicial conscience should it be held that the jury has acted out of passion or prejudice and that the award is disproportionate.

Nature of the Wrongful Act Some jurisdictions rule that the amount of punitive damages awarded should be based upon the degree of culpability of the wrongdoer and the nature and reprehensibility of the act or acts complained of. Culpability and the nature of the act(s), according to these courts, has definite bearing on the correctness of a jury award. In addition, placing emphasis on the enormity of the wrong and the necessity of preventing similar wrong justifies a jury award that serves not only to punish the wrongdoer, but also serves as a deterrent to others that are similarly minded.

A Delaware court considered the nature and reprehensibility of the act and concluded that the magnitude of the jury award was completely inappropriate, suggesting that the jury was moved by impermissible passion or prejudice. In other cases, courts have permitted the jury award to stand because the defendant was guilty of acts of such wrongful and reprehensible nature that the jury awards seemed appropriate.

Financial Status or Wealth of Defendant However, some plaintiffs' attorneys have failed to present evidence concerning the financial ability of the defendant to pay the award. As a consequence, jury awards of punitive damages have been held to be excessive because of the lack of such evidence. Courts determine that without such evidence there is no guide whereby the jury can determine punitive damages. Other courts have held to the contrary.

Since punitive damages are made to punish as well as to act as a deterrent to further wrongful conduct, the financial status or wealth of the defendant is certainly relevant. A California court in 1981 ruled that the wealth of the defendant may be considered, observing that an award which is so small that it can be simply written off as part of the cost of doing business would have no deterring effect. On the other hand, an award which affects the company's pricing of its products thereby affecting its competitive advantage, would serve as a deterrent.

A 1974 Missouri case also considered the financial circumstance of the defendant. Since punitive damages have been referred to as "smart" money, it takes only slight consideration to realize that an amount of damages which might "smart" one defendant, might be entirely inconsequential to another. In this case, the court ruled that the punitive damage award was exceedingly small when comparing the award to the defendant's net worth.

Other Factors Affecting Awards   Other factors that may have an important bearing upon the amount of punitive damages awarded and sustained by courts are such things as the amount allowed as punishment in similar cases, statutes which limit the amount of the award, and the fine or penalty applicable in a criminal action for the same or similar offense.

A number of courts have ruled that punitive damages cannot exceed the amount specified under federal or state statutes. We can anticipate that there will be more of these types of rulings, since states have recently enacted statutes that restrict the amount of punitive damages that may be awarded.

There are various services that study and accumulate statistics regarding typical jury verdicts on various types of personal injuries and wrongful deaths. These can serve as a guide in determining what is an appropriate claims payment to be made in a specific case. A number of courts have ruled that similar cases can establish a precedent for jury awards in punitive damages. Thus, you would be wise to have access to these services that give you some guidance on valuations of claims. Your supervisor and company claims examiners will provide you with helpful guidance in claims evaluations.

Inadequacy and Excessiveness Cases

Some large jury verdicts have been reduced substantially by courts when it has appeared that the jury verdict has been disproportionately generous. On the other hand, there have been cases where the court has ruled that the award is not excessive. Examination of some of these cases may prove to be instructive, particularly where the judge provides sound reasoning for a verdict revision.

In one case, the plaintiff sustained burns when he was sprayed with gasoline from the tank of a tractor. Evidence showed that the manufacturer's personnel were alerted to potential problems with fuel tank vent holes but took no action to correct the problem; yet the judge reduced the jury's verdict from $7,500,000 to $650,000 in this case. The judge's reasoning was unclear, but he obviously believed the verdict to be excessive.

In another case, $1 million was awarded to an eighty-four-year-old claimant against a cosmetic manufacturer where the claimant alleged the use of the manufacturer's skin cream had afflicted her with mercury poisoning. The court noted that the claimant had a life expectancy of 8.3 years and had a medical history of multiple physical ailments. The judge noted that the case was rife with a potential that the jury might allow sympathy for her experience to insinuate itself to a considerable degree into the deliberation and awarding of damages. Thus, the judge ordered a new trial.

In another case, two men were killed when a fuel tank on a truck tractor manufactured by the defendant ruptured and ignited. Compensatory damages were awarded in the amount of $150,000; however punitive damages of $10 million were awarded by the jury. Noting that the punitive damage award was sixty-seven times the size of the compensatory damage award, the judge ordered a new trial.

On the other hand, a number of cases have been reported where the judge ruled that the jury verdict was not excessive. In the 1981 *Grimshaw v. Ford Motor Co.* case some $3,500,000 was awarded the plaintiff against Ford Motor for injuries suffered due to a design defect, an exploding gasoline tank that ruptured in rear-end collisions.[14] The judge noted that Ford Motor had assets of $7,700,000,000 and its income after taxes for the year in question was over $983,000,000. Thus, the court noted that the punitive award was approximately .005 percent of the company's net worth and approximately .3 percent of its net income.

A number of cases in which the court ruled punitive damages were not excessive would arouse the sympathy of even the most callous reader. An example is a 1980 Minnesota case in which $1 million in punitive damages was awarded a four-year-old child who sustained second and third degree burns over 20% of her body, resulting in permanent disfigurement, because her "flannelette" pajamas caught fire when she stood too close to a stove.

In another case, an award of $100,000 was granted in punitive damages in a wrongful death action against the driver of an automobile which struck the plaintiff's husband while he was pouring gasoline into his disabled truck. The defendant in this case was intoxicated at the time of the accident.

COMPARATIVE NEGLIGENCE REDUCING PUNITIVE DAMAGES

The doctrine of comparative negligence, which has usually been established by statute, provides that, at least in some cases, the contributory negligency of the person injured will not be a complete bar to recovery but there will be an apportionment of responsibility, or of damages, in accordance with the relative fault of the persons involved.

The courts have been at odds in determining whether comparative negligence should have any bearing upon the amount of punitive damages awarded. Some courts have ruled that punitive or exemplary damages recoverable by a plaintiff should not be reduced by the percentage of the plaintiff's negligence. For example, a 1973 Florida court judge held that the comparative negligence doctrine could not be used to reduce the amount of punitive damages by the percentage of the plaintiff's contributory negligence. The court stated that the comparative negligence doctrine would be invoked to offset the negligence claims made against the defendants, but observed that a further problem arose where, as in the instant case, gross negligence of the defendant was alleged. In such a situation, the equitable course, according to the judge, was to allow the plaintiff's negligence to diminish its recovery of compensatory damages.

However, if gross negligence of the defendants supported an award of punitive damages, the court held that the amount of the exemplary award would not be diminished by the amount of the plaintiff's negligence. The court stated that reducing the amount of compensatory damages by the percentage of the plaintiff's negligence while refusing to reduce the punitive damages by the same percentage would equitably divide responsibility for claimed losses while keeping intact the underlying policy of punitive damages—punishing wanton acts.

In a similar case, a federal court in Oklahoma in 1980 declared that while it was required to construe the comparative negligence statute of the state of Oklahoma, an award of punitive or exemplary damages could not be reduced by the percentage of negligence of the plaintiff. Stating that punitive damages are in the nature of punishment imposed for the benefit of society as a restraint upon the transgressor and as a warning and example to deter others, the court reasoned that this policy would be violated if punitive or exemplary damages were allowed to be reduced by the amount of the plaintiff's contributory negligence.

These courts in refusing to apply the doctrine of comparative negligence to punitive damages have recognized that punitive damages are awarded for quasi-criminal conduct, and where the plaintiff is not guilty of wanton and malicious acts, it would be inappropriate to likewise punish the plaintiff by offsetting part of the award due the plaintiff by the defendant arising out of the defendant's wanton and malicious acts.

Nevertheless, the courts are inconsistent on this point. A Texas court in 1979 allowed the reduction of a punitive damage award by the percentage of the plaintiff's negligence.[15]

PUNITIVE DAMAGES FOR FAILURE TO SETTLE CLAIMS

While liability insurance policies ordinarily reserve to the insurer the decision whether an offer to compromise a claim against the insured should be settled, it is quite clear today that a greater duty is imposed upon insurers to consider the insured's best interests at least equally with those of the insurance company when it comes to making a settlement decision.

The courts are not in agreement regarding the granting of punitive damages for failure to settle a claim, and different results have been reached with regard to the recoverability of punitive damages. However, the trend is definitely toward showing more sympathy to the insured.

Where insureds have brought actions to recover punitive or exemplary damages from their automobile liability insurers for failing to settle claims against insureds, a number of courts have permitted an award of such damages where the insurers acted maliciously, wantonly, recklessly, deceptively, or in bad faith toward their insureds. For example, where the automobile insurers not only failed to accept settlement offers which were within the limits of the liability policies, but also concealed from their insureds the fact that the offers of settlement had been tendered, or deliberately misinformed the insureds concerning the content of such offers, punitive damages have been held to be recoverable by the insureds.

Additionally, punitive damages were imposed on an insurer which rejected an offer to settle within the liability limits even though it realized that the injuries sustained by the claimant were so severe that were liability established against the insured, the damages assessed would greatly exceed the insurance policy limits, exhaust the insured's personal assets, and force him into bankruptcy.

On the other hand, courts have been lenient towards insurers when, in contrast to the previous mentioned instances of active misrepresentation and active concealment, the insurers either just completely ignored their insured's case, or negligently failed to accept settlement offers, or failed to make any counteroffers. These courts reasoned that the insurers had been guilty neither of gross negligence nor of a continued course of dishonest dealing, thus punitive damages were not recoverable. Similarly, where insurers, in refusing to accept claimants' settlement offers, have stubbornly or unreasonably disregarded the advice of their own agents and attorneys to settle, or had merely bungled a claim by having tried to handle it under an inappropriate provision of the policy, some courts have refused to impose damages because the insurers' personnel have not been actuated by malice, bad faith, or a reckless disregard for the rights of the insured.

In addition, some courts have stated that in the absence of a finding that the insurer acted wantonly, maliciously, or in bad faith toward the insured, punitive damages would not be assessed against an insurer even if, in refusing to accept settlement offers within the limits of insurance coverage, the insurer had (1) failed to follow the settlement recommendations of its agents and attorneys, and (2) failed to properly consider the interests of the insured.

It is true that some jurisdictions do not recognize awards of punitive damages. It is further true that some courts interpret punitive damage law in a way similar to that of the judicial reasoning of Chief Justice Rehnquist, requiring culpability and intentionally injurious conduct. As a matter of warning, however, it is not erroneous to predict that courts will be more liberal toward plaintiffs in future years, and even at the present time punitive damages are being awarded in many cases for claims handling that is merely sloppy, inefficient, careless, forgetful, or negligent. The safest rule to follow is that any negligent conduct can result in a lawsuit that may culminate in punitive or exemplary damages being awarded.

NEED FOR ACTUAL DAMAGES

As a general rule, courts have held that punitive damages may not be awarded unless the party seeking them has sustained actual damages. Nevertheless, this is not a universal rule, and we noted that the U.S. Supreme Court in a 1980 decision ruled that "punitive damages may be the only significant remedy available where constitutional rights are maliciously violated but the victim cannot prove compensable injury.[16]

Nevertheless, the courts in some jurisdictions have taken the view that there must be a finding and award of actual or compensatory damages before an award of punitive damages may be made. Exceptions are made in torts where general damages are inherent or presumed. For example, courts in at least ten states, in addition to federal courts, have held that in actions for libel or slander based on language that is defamatory per se, proof of the libel or slander creates a presumption that some actual damage has been sustained, even though it is incapable of measurement. The presumption eliminates the need to show actual damages before a punitive damage award may be made. Other courts have taken the view that the important factor is the sustaining of the legal injury, rather than its monetary assessment. Thus, a showing of an invasion of a legal right is sufficient to support an award of punitive damages. Recently state and federal cases have permitted awards of punitive damages without the proof of actual or compensatory damages. In a 1979 Iowa case, an award of $2,500 punitive damages was ruled proper in a breach of contract case where the court found an intentional tort maliciously committed, although the plaintiff was unable to prove the amount of his actual damages. In a 1983 Montana case, the court affirmed an award of $30,000 punitive damages against an insurer for failure to settle promptly a claim on which liability had become reasonably clear even though the jury made no award for compensatory damages. Federal courts in Wisconsin, Illinois, and New York have made similar rulings.

About all that can be said in this particular subject area is that the law is in a state of flux, and no general conclusions can be reached regarding whether punitive damages can be awarded if there are no compensatory damages shown. The safest rule to follow is to examine the law in the particular jurisdiction in which the matter arises.

INSURANCE PROTECTION FOR PUNITIVE DAMAGES

With the expansion of the large jury verdicts granted in punitive damage cases, together with an increased frequency of such cases, there was a natural desire of insurers to attempt to obtain a judicial determination that punitive damages fell outside of the liability insurance policy coverage. Without question, the insuring agreement of the standard liability policy provides coverage for compensatory damages for which the insured becomes liable. But the coverage issue becomes less clear when applied to the area of punitive damages settlement. Are insurance companies obligated to pay the punitive damages incurred by their insureds? There is no single answer.[17]

Five Positions Applicable on Punitive Damages

One excellent source of information on the subject of punitive damages is the *FC&S Bulletins*, published by the National Underwriter Company. The *FC&S Bulletins* state that any one of five positions may be applicable relative to the awarding of punitive damages or insurance covering them. It depends upon the particular jurisdiction since some state statutes or judicial decisions in those states bar punitive damages, or public policy considerations rule out the possibility of punitive damages.

The five positions applicable regarding punitive damages are as follows:

1. State law or judicial interpretation may not allow punitive damage awards at all;

2. Punitive damage awards may be permitted and, so too, recovery of punitive damages under liability policies;
3. Punitive damage awards may be permitted but insurance against them prohibited as contrary to public policy;
4. Insurance may be allowed in some circumstances but not others (as in Missouri, where, contrary to the general policy of the state, police officers' punitive damages are insurable); or
5. The situation may be yet undecided in the state in which the claim originates.[18]

In short, the *FC&S Bulletins* conclude that one cannot make any general statements regarding punitive damages, since the situation is in a state of flux. Court decisions add to the diversity of position rather than strengthening a particular view, though recent cases tend to support the insurability of punitive damages.

Current State of the Law

As of April 1984, some twenty-one states had held punitive damage awards insurable; fifteen states and the District of Columbia had ruled that they were uninsurable, usually as "against public policy"; and ten states were undetermined. Four states—Louisiana, Massachusetts, Nebraska, and Washington—and Puerto Rico recognized no form of punitive damages, thereby negating the insurability issue. Three other states—Connecticut, Michigan, and New Hampshire—excluded awards for punitive damages per se. The *FC&S Bulletins* provide an excellent tabular summary of the status of punitive damages by state, together with court citations.[19]

Again, one must be aware of the fact that this whole area of bad faith, punitive damages, and unfair claims settlement practices statutes is in an unsettled state. Changes are occurring rapidly and today's publications on this subject matter are usually outdated by tomorrow. The only safe course of conduct for you to follow is to make certain that you have the latest legal information on a subject before relying upon dated materials. One thing that is certain and that remains constant is the opposition of the insurance industry toward having to insure against punitive damages. There are two strong reasons advanced by insurers against the insuring of punitive damages—(1) punitive damages result from an intentional act, and therefore should not be insurable and (2) insuring against punitive damages which arise out of a quasi-criminal act is surely against public policy. These arguments will be discussed in the following sections.

Argument—Punitive Damages
Result from an Intentional Act

There was a natural inclination on the part of insurers to defend against punitive damage awards under their liability policies, since liability insurance is supposed to cover accidental conduct. At least, the conduct is supposed to be accidental from the standpoint of the insured.

A number of liability insurance policies provide coverage against intentional acts, not arising out of intentional conduct of the insured but committed by the insured's employees, agents or children. In addition, there is liability exposure from vicarious or imputed liability situations where an insured can be responsible for an intentional act because of a special statutory liability or contractual liability. Furthermore, there are liability policies that are designed to cover intentional acts such as those policies designed to cover libel, slander, or defamation.

These types of situations where an insurer grants liability insurance coverage for intentional acts make it difficult for insurers to argue that a liability policy does not cover punitive damages arising out of conduct that would otherwise appear to be intentional. Furthermore, in jurisdictions that award punitive damages in cases involving neglect or gross negligence or similar acts or omissions, the question of intent is irrelevant. Another complicating factor, of course, is that many of the cases are brought directly against the insurance company.

A federal court in Delaware in 1986 expressed the general rule regarding the exclusion of punitive damages under a liability policy.[20] The court reasoned that the policy language obligating the insurer to "pay damages for bodily injury or property damage" was ambiguous and should be interpreted to include punitive damages. The court also expressed the opinion that the policy's intentional act exclusion did not preclude coverage of punitive damages. Again construing the policy against the insurer, the court concluded that the intentional act exclusion should not be read to exclude coverage for the type of gross, wanton, or reckless negligence on which the punitive damage award was based.

Argument—Punitive Damages
Coverage Against Public Policy

The federal court in Delaware also addressed the question of whether insurance coverage of punitive damages is contrary to public policy. Emphasizing the importance of the right to contract, the court declared that the right should not be undermined unless it violates some clearly stated public policy. Indeed, the court concluded that

Delaware's mandatory automobile liability law demonstrated a public policy in favor of insurance coverage for punitive damages.

Nevertheless, there is a decided split of authority on whether public policy permits insurance coverage of punitive damages. Almost half of the states allow insurance coverage of punitive damages.

Other states have held that public policy permits insurance coverage of punitive damages where the insured is a government entity. The reason for these decisions is usually that non-coverage would have a "chilling effect" on the acts of government employees. This means they would avoid any situation that might lead to a punitive damage situation, even if it meant shirking their responsibilities to serve the public. This, of course, would not be in the public interest.

In addition, those states which allow coverage of punitive damages generally also allow it where liability is imposed by reason of the doctrine of respondeat superior—liability of employer for the acts of an agent, for example. Similarly, a number of jurisdictions hold that there is insurance coverage for punitive damages where liability is vicarious.

Some nine or ten states have declared that persons may not insure for punitive damages. Finally, there are ten or eleven jurisdictions that have not decided the issue, either because there is no ruling statute on the point or else a court has not acted as yet.[21]

California and New York have held, as a matter of public policy, that punitive damages are not insurable. The rationale for providing insurability of punitive damages is best set forth in the decision of the New York Court of Appeals, which denies coverage:

> The arguments for allowing coverage are that the number of instances in which punitive damages are awarded shows that they are not really a deterrent, that coverage does not eliminate deterrence in any event because the cost of such insurance and of the possibility of added premium loading for any insured for whom a carrier is required to pay punitive damages, that the policy language is broad enough to cover both compensatory and punitive damages and would be so interpreted by the average policy holder, particularly since small businesses can be wiped out by such an award, and that even those courts which do hold that public policy proscribes coverage do not void coverage of punitive damages payable by defendants held liable only vicariously.[22]

Despite its statement of the arguments for allowing coverage, New York refuses to insure punitive damages—on public policy grounds.

CONCLUSION

The subject of punitive or exemplary damages presents an area of liability which is extremely dangerous for insurers and claims adjusters alike. Insurance adjusters should derive some comfort from the knowledge that they cannot be held responsible in contract for the contractual obligations of their employers. However, tort liability is another matter. Adjusters can escape contract liability because they are the agents of a disclosed principal. But if an adjuster commits a tort on behalf of an employer, the adjuster is jointly and severally liable for that wrong.

Ordinarily, adjusters did not have to worry about tort liability while working for an insurance company because of the "deep pockets" phenomenon: the plaintiff pursued the defendant that had the greatest ability to pay. Adjusters were usually ignored. Today, however, with the abolition or modification of the joint and several liability rule in a number of the states, the potential of becoming *personally* liable on a large jury verdict for punitive damages is a major worry.

When the foregoing is considered together with the fact that the whole area of bad faith law, punitive damages, and unfair claim settlement practices liability seems to be expanding, it is apparent that the area of insurance claims adjusting is faced with some peril. The standard of conduct today is a demanding one.

Consequently, it is incumbent upon adjusters to act in a manner that will keep them out of trouble and keep them out of court. This requires that adjusters perform as reasonable, prudent people. William L. Prosser wrote:

> The courts have dealt with this very difficult problem by creating a fictitious person, who never has existed on land or sea.... The actor is required to do what such an ideal individual would be supposed to do in his place. A model of all proper qualities, with only those human shortcomings and weaknesses which the community will tolerate on the occasion, "this excellent but odious character stands like a monument in our Courts of Justice, vainly appealing to his fellow-citizens to order their lives after his own example.... He is an ideal, a standard, the embodiment of all those qualities which we demand of the good citizen.... He is one who invariably looks where he is going and is careful to examine the immediate foreground before he executes a leap or a bound; who neither star-gazes nor is lost in meditation when approaching trap-doors or the margin of a dock;...who never mounts a moving omnibus and does not alight from any car while the train is in motion...and will inform himself of the history and habits of a dog before administering a caress;...who never drives his ball until those in front of him have definitely vacated the putting-green which is his own objective; who never from one year's end to another makes an excessive demand upon his wife, his neighbors, his servants, his ox, or his ass;...who never swears, gambles, or loses his temper; who uses nothing except in moderation, and even while he flogs his child is meditating only on the golden mean.[23]

Chapter Notes

1. William L. Prosser, *Handbook of the Law of Torts* (St. Paul, MN: West Publishing Co., 1941), pp. 11-12.
2. *Temmen v. Kent-Brown Chevrolet Co.*, 227 Kan. 45, 605 P.2d 95 (1980).
3. *Guarantee Abstract v. Interstate Fire & Casualty*, 232 Kan. 76, 652 P.2d 665 (1982).
4. *Lipinski v. Title Insurance Co.*, 655 P.2d 970 (Mont. 1982).
5. Prosser, p. 13.
6. *Carlson v. Green*, 446 U.S. 14 at 22 n. 9, 100 Sup.Ct. 1468 at 1473, n. 9.
7. Prosser, p. 29.
8. *Taylor v. Superior Court*, 24 Cal. 3rd 890 (1974).
9. Victor B. Levit, "Recent Developments in Bad Faith and Punitive Damages," *CPCU Journal*, V. 38 (March 1985), p. 32.
10. *Smith v. Wade*, 461 U.S. 30, 103 S. Ct. Rptr. 1625, 75 L.Ed. 2d 632 (1983).
11. *Welch v. Durand*, 36 Conn. 182 (1869).
12. *Day v. Woodworth*, 13 How. 363, 371, 14 L.Ed. 181 (1852).
13. *Christy v. Butcher*, 153 Mo. App. 397, 401, 134 SW 1058, 1059 (1911).
14. *Grimshaw v. Ford Motor Co.*, 119 Cal. App. 3rd 757, 174 Cal. Rptr. 348 (Cal. 4th Dist., 1981).
15. *Pedernales Electric Cooperative, Inc. v. Schulz*, 588 S.W. 2d 882 (Tex. Civ. App. 10th Dist., 1979).
16. *Carlson v. Green*, 446 U.S. 14 at 22, n. 9, 100 S. Ct. 1468 at 1473, n. 9.
17. "Punitive Damages," *FC&S Bulletins*—Casualty and Surety (The National Underwriter, April, 1984), Public Liability Coda-1.
18. "Punitive Damages," *FC&S Bulletins*—Casualty and Surety (The National Underwriter, April, 1984), Public Liability Coda-1.
19. "Punitive Damages," *FC&S Bulletins* (National Underwriter, May, 1985), Public Liability Coda-2 and Coda-3 (the second page is dated February, 1986).
20. *Valley Forge Insurance Co. v. Jefferson*, 628 F.Supp. 502 (Del. 1986).
21. For an excellent jurisdictional survey of the present state of the law regarding the insurability of punitive damages, see *Insurance Litigation Reporter* (June 1986), pp. 1033-1036.
22. *Hartford Accident and Indemnity Co. v. Village of Hempstead*, 48 New York 2d 218 (N.Y. 1979).
23. Prosser, pp. 225-226.

CHAPTER 4

Unfair Claims Settlement Practices Statutes

Most major industries in the United States are regulated by some federal agency. For example, the energy industry is regulated by the Federal Energy Regulatory Commission. The broadcasting industry is regulated by the Federal Communications Commission. Most work places in America are regulated by the Occupational Safety and Health Administration. The securities industry, one in which the insurance industry is becoming more and more involved, is regulated by the Securities and Exchange Commission, and so forth.

Why don't we have a federal agency that performs the major regulatory function for the insurance industry? Given the pattern of regulation in the United States, one would expect to find that a major industry as important as the insurance business would be regulated by some federal agency, such as a federal insurance regulatory commission. This is not the case, however. There is no federal insurance regulatory commission. The regulatory system of the insurance industry is completely different from that of other major industries, and the reason is largely a matter of historical accident.

CONSTITUTIONAL INTRODUCTION—HISTORY

To understand the reason why insurance is not under heavy federal regulation requires some examination of history. You must understand the relation between the federal and state governments in order to understand what happened. The pattern of insurance regulation was established shortly after the Civil War. But let us examine the legal foundation for the regulation of any type of business in the United States. To do this, we must look at the U. S. Constitution.

Federal Power to Regulate "Commerce"

Article 1, Section 8 of the U. S. Constitution provides that "the Congress shall have the power...to regulate Commerce with foreign Nations, and among the several States, and with the Indian tribes; ...." Today, one would surely expect that the insurance industry is certainly "commerce." However, back in the nineteenth century, the federal courts were not certain on that point. This was because of a very narrow construction, or interpretation, of the Constitution.

The United States Supreme Court during the nineteenth century seemed to be somewhat capricious in its interpretation of what was meant by the word "commerce." The Court first defined the word in the case of *Gibbons v. Ogden* in 1824.[1] Commerce, said Justice Marshall, "is traffic, but it is something more...It describes the commercial intercourse between nations and parts of nations, in all its branches...." One would expect that such a broad definition would extend beyond the act of buying and selling across state lines. In other words, it would include all the processes through which trade is carried on. It surely would appear that insurance should be included within the sweep of such broad Supreme Court language. However, that is not the way it worked in the case of the insurance industry.

Early State Regulation

Early in the nineteenth century some states attempted to regulate the insurance business through placing restrictive provision in charters issued to insurers. These charters regulated such things as investments, reserve requirements, and limitations on the type of insurance that could be offered by an insurance company. Some charters required the insurers to report on their financial condition. Massachusetts required publication of annual reports as early as 1818. Other states soon followed with similar regulations and also required companies from out of state to file financial statements within those states in which they were operating. Thus, a company in New York would be required to file financial information if it wished to do business in the state of Virginia. New Hampshire established the first separate insurance commission in 1851, and other states soon followed.

Canada had been employing a dual system of regulation. The Dominion of Canada (the federal government) supervised insurance solvency, and the various provinces (states) regulated contract provisions, agent licensing, and general insurer operations.

The U. S. House of Representatives in 1862 introduced a bill to create a national Bureau of Insurance in the Treasury Department. The U. S. Senate introduced a similar bill in 1868. Both proposals were defeated.[2] The matter was resolved in 1868 in the famous insurance case of *Paul v. Virginia.*

Paul v. Virginia

Samuel Paul of Virginia was an agent for some New York insurance companies. In order to write insurance in the state of Virginia, that state required New York insurers to post a security deposit before the state of Virginia would issue a license. Sam refused to make the deposit and began to sell fire insurance without a license. He was subsequently arrested, convicted, and fined $50. The case finally reached the U. S. Supreme Court, and the Court stated:

> Issuing a policy of insurance is not a transaction of commerce. . .These contracts are not articles of commerce in any proper meaning of the word. . .they are not commodities to be shipped or forwarded from one State to another and then put up for sale. . . .Such contracts are not interstate transactions. . . .[3]

Curiously, however, the Court decided that transport and communications were under federal jurisdiction in cases decided in 1872 and 1877.[4]

Insurance was not declared to be "commerce" by the Supreme Court until 1944. During the seventy-five years in which insurance was outside the realm of interstate commerce, other commercial activities were rapidly being interpreted as belonging under the jurisdiction of the federal government. During the same period of time, insurers continued to challenge *Paul v. Virginia* in the hope that they could escape what they thought to be onerous state regulations.

Finally, in 1942, the Antitrust Division of the U.S. Department of Justice challenged the judicial precedent of *Paul v. Virginia* and attempted to apply the Sherman Antitrust Act to the business of insurance. This resulted in the landmark insurance decision of the *U. S. v. South-Eastern Underwriters Association* case.

U. S. v. SEUA

The South-Eastern Underwriters Association controlled 90 percent of the fire insurance and allied lines business in its area and was accused of restraining interstate commerce by fixing and maintaining arbitrary and noncompetitive premium rates on fire and allied lines in the Southeast and also monopolizing commerce in insurance. The Association was also charged with fixing agents' commissions, using boycotts, and compelling prospective insurers to buy only from SEUA members on SEUA terms.

In the case before the federal district court, the Association claimed that regardless of its conduct, it was not subject to federal law. The lower court upheld this viewpoint and dismissed the case, using *Paul v. Virginia* as the prevailing federal law. On appeal to the United States Supreme Court, the decision was reversed, and the Supreme Court held that insurance is interstate commerce when it traverses state lines and is therefore subject to federal antitrust law. The Court stated:

> No commercial enterprise of any kind which conducts its activities across state lines has been held to be wholly beyond the regulatory power of Congress under the Commerce Clause. We cannot make an exception of the business of insurance.[5]

Significance of **Paul v. Virginia**   The fact that insurance was exempted from federal regulation at such an early date in the development of the U. S. insurance business was highly significant in establishing a pattern of government regulation that has become more or less permanent. *Paul v. Virginia* established the supremacy of the states to regulate insurance. Thus, over a period of seventy-five years many states developed strong insurance departments, and all states provided for the regulation of insurance. A large amount of state legislation was enacted regulating most of the activities of insurance. The business was considered to be "affected with a public interest." In other words, it was in the public interest to make certain that insurance companies behaved in a responsible manner. This pattern of state insurance regulation set the stage for insurance company operations, and many large states, particularly New York, contributed to the standarization of insurance company policies, practices, and regulations.

State Insurance Commissioners and the NAIC   Each state has an insurance regulatory official that has the primary responsibility to regulate insurance activities within a given state. In most states, the head of the department bears the title of Insurance Commissioner or Commissioner of Insurance, although in several states the individual is titled "Superintendent of Insurance" or "Director of Insurance." In a few states, the responsibility of regulating the state insurance business is held by some elected official who bears another title, and insurance regulation is sort of an adjunct responsibility of the elected office. In most cases, however, the Insurance Commissioner is an appointed individual.

In 1871 the heads of the various state insurance departments formed a voluntary organization known as the National Convention of Insurance Commissioners. The name was subsequently changed to the National Association of Insurance Commissioners (NAIC). By 1944, the NAIC had become highly instrumental in adopting uniform policies and procedures and model legislation which the individual commissioners then encouraged their individual state legislatures to enact for application in their respective states.

Confusion Created by the SEUA Case   Understandably, when the Supreme Court first declared that insurance was interstate commerce and subject to federal regulation in the 1944 SEUA case, both the state regulatory commissioners and the federal government experienced considerable dismay and bewilderment. The states historically had provided for insurance regulation. They had insurance departments and a large body of legislation and administrative rules and regulations dealing with and regulating the insurance business. The federal government, on the other hand, in 1944 had no regulatory apparatus to conduct that regulatory responsibility.

The states did not wish to lose their regulatory authority, and the federal government was not keen on assuming that authority. To resolve the matter, Congress enacted the McCarran-Ferguson Act— Public Law 15 in 1945.

McCarran-Ferguson Act—Public Law 15   The McCarran-Ferguson Act specifically exempted insurers from the major antitrust laws until July of 1948, when the antitrust acts became applicable to insurance if not regulated by state law. The states had to comply with the spirit and substance of federal antitrust philosophy. They were given three years in which to enact state antitrust laws that would comply with the federal directive. If the states failed to comply, the federal government threatened to regulate the insurance industry to the extent that the states failed to regulate.[6]

Responding to the federal threat, the National Association of Insurance Commissioners, together with industry representatives, developed a Model Unfair Trade Practices bill. By the deadline in 1948, all of the states had enacted the NAIC Model bill, either in whole or in part, in order to escape federal regulations. This Model bill satisfactorily met the regulatory standards required by the McCarran-Ferguson Act—Public Law 15.

THE STATE UNFAIR TRADE PRACTICES ACTS

The NAIC Model Unfair Trade Practices bill defined unfair methods of competition or unfair or deceptive acts. Misconduct included misrepresentation, false advertising, defamation, boycott, coercion, intimidation, false financial statements, questionable stock operations and advisory board contracts, unfair pricing discrimination in life and health insurance, and commission rebates to buyers.[7] These practices were not exhaustive, and they were not intended to limit the powers of the state insurance departments. However, reference to insurance claims-handling practices was not specifically included in the Unfair Trade Practices legislation.

Exclusivity of Administrative Remedy

There was a strong contention expressed in a number of court rulings that the Unfair Trade Practices legislation of the 1940s provided exclusivity of remedy in the state insurance departments. In other words, private individuals had no right of action under the legislation. Courts held in a number of occasions that the 1940s state legislation was drafted to follow the legislative intent of the federal lawmakers when Congress enacted the Federal Trade Commission (FTC) Act in 1914, together with its amendments, and the Sherman Act of 1890, together with its amendments. Some federal court cases have ruled that no private right of action was created under the Federal Trade Commission Act.[8]

There is a strong argument that the NAIC drafters borrowed the form of the FTC Act to create the same legislation at the state level. Therefore, it is argued that the interpretation of the FTC Act by the federal judiciary would be demonstrative of the intent of the drafters and legislatures, both federal and state. The contention is made that the federal courts have consistently held that the FTC Act, as amended, does not create by implication a private cause of action for unfair or deceptive practices.

The theory is interesting; however, like all theories it has experienced revision and attack. The FTC Act enacted in 1914 dates from an era of relatively unbridled "laissez-faire" government. In 1914, little emphasis was placed on the matter of consumer protection (the new Food and Drug Act of 1906 being a notable exception).

Some States Provide Private Rights of Action

Progressive, people-oriented judicial thinking has had a marked influence on litigation for the past several decades. Times change. Courts interpret statutes in light of social conditions that exist today. Increased public expectations and awareness and the emphasis upon expanded consumer protection has had a marked impact. Insurance contracts have been interpreted to favor the insured, particularly in cases where ambiguity exists in the drafting of the policy. Recent cases have declared that private individuals *do* have private rights under the state unfair trade practices laws.

For example, a federal court in Louisiana ruled that the State

Unfair Trades Practices Act does not give the state insurance department exclusivity of remedy:

> ...it seems inescapable that the Louisiana legislature did not intend to make action by the Commissioner of Insurance the sole remedy for a violation of Section 1213. The Insurance Code defines the obligation of an insurer in terms of such magnitude as to describe a legal duty to provide truthful, accurate information to policy holders beyond whatever action the Commissioner is empowered to take.[9]

Maine declares under Section 207 of Title 5, Chapter 10, that "unfair methods of competition and unfair or deceptive acts or practices in the conduct of any trade or commerce are declared unlawful." It then states that the intent of the legislature in construing this section is to be guided by the interpretations given by the FTC and the federal courts to the FTC Act. It then contradicts itself in Section 213, where Maine legislators specifically authorize private remedies, allowing an action for restitution and for such other equitable relief, including an injunction, as the courts may deem to be necessary and proper.[10] A Maine court acknowledges the uniqueness of Section 213 and points out that federal decisions interpreting the FTC Act "afford uncertain guidance in the interpretation of the Maine private remedial provisions."[11]

Texas provides private rights of action under its Unfair Trade Practices Act.[12] Recent cases recognize that private rights do exist.[13]

Federal Assaults on the State Unfair Trade Practices Laws

The federal government has intervened in the insurance business in some cases even though states have enacted unfair trade practices laws. Where state law is ineffective in regulating an alleged abuse, federal regulatory agencies have intervened. For example, the Federal Trade Commission issued complaints against forty-one insurance companies, stating that their health insurance advertising violated the Federal Trade Commission Act. The U. S. Supreme Court ruled that the FTC has jurisdiction over those insurers using direct mail advertising where state insurance laws are impotent to regulate any alleged misconduct or where the insurers' activity is held not to be connected with the "business of insurance."[14]

The U. S. Department of Justice has also exerted its jurisdiction in cases involving mergers, boycotts, coercion, and intimidation.[15] Again, the federal government intervenes where state regulation does not adequately cover the situation.

The jurisdiction of the Securities and Exchange Commission over the business of insurance was upheld by the U. S. Supreme Court when it ruled that the Securities Act of 1933 and the Investment Company Act of 1940 applied to insurers selling variable annuity contracts.[16] Variable annuities are regulated as securities, since they are based upon a common stock account.[17] Variable life insurance policies are similarly regulated by the SEC under regulations drafted with the aid and cooperation of the NAIC.

THE UNFAIR CLAIMS SETTLEMENT PRACTICES ACTS

The state unfair trade practices laws were adequate to protect the public from abuses in most insurer/insuring-public circumstances. However, during the ensuing years the area of insurance claims handling came under increasing criticism, spawning a body of "bad faith" litigation against insurers that arose out of alleged unfair claims settlement practices.

It was standard practice not too many years ago for many claims departments not to stir up any quiescent claims, whether they were first-party or third-party claims.[18] Further, delay was an effective technique in holding down claims costs. Although these practices were appropriate strategies in cases of doubtful or disputed liability, they were viewed as unconscionable conduct by the public and by many insurers in those cases involving clear-cut liability to insurers or third-party claimants. Moreover, the insurance industry's public image was tarnished when, in a few cases, claims departments were instructed to deny all claims irrespective of merit.

The New York Statute

Responding to public complaints, the state of New York enacted legislation in 1970 to protect consumers by authorizing sanctions and penalties against insurers engaged in improper claims practices. Section 40-d of the New York Insurance Law is titled "Unfair Claims Settlement Practices by Insurers." The statute reads:

> No insurer doing business in the state shall engage in unfair claims settlement practices. Any of the following acts by an insurer, if committed without just cause and performed with such frequency as to indicate a general business practice, shall constitute unfair claims settlement practices. . . .[19]

The statute then goes on to list those claims-handling practices considered to be unfair and illegal.

The New York law established the name for the new body of legislation and initiated a flurry of state legislation nationwide dealing with unfair claims practices. When the New York legislature enacted its 1970 law, it sought to establish higher standards for insurer and insuring-public relations, to facilitate better communication between the parties, and to provide a range of sanctions that could be used against those insurers who consistently overstepped the boundaries of socially responsible and legally acceptable corporate behavior.

Another NAIC Model Act

It was well recognized that the new legislation in New York would exert a compelling influence on other states. Something had to be done to guide the expected reaction of other states' legislatures. Spurred by the new New York law, the National Association of Insurance Commissioners in 1971 and 1972 reviewed its 1945 Model Act dealing with unfair trade practices and incorporated a new Section 9, commonly referred to as the "Unfair Claims Settlement Practices Act," designed to establish standards for the proper handling of insurance claims. Almost all states now have incorporated in whole or in part the provisions of Section 9 of the NAIC Model Act.

Nature of the Model Act The Model Act is essentially a fourteen-part Declaration of Misconduct in insurance claims handling. It is a codification of certain offenses, some of which may also become "bad faith" problems if done to harm a claimant or done with malice or reckless disregard for a claimant's rights. The requirements of the new act place great emphasis on the following:

1. The "Immediate Contact Rule"
2. Timely and Continual Communication
3. Diligence
4. Honesty
5. Fairness
6. Reasonableness

The "immediate contact rule" is highly important in the new Act. The provisions of the Act emphatically stress timely and continual communication and the absolute necessity for honesty and fairness. The standard of reasonableness which must be met is that which one would require of a "reasonable man (person)."

The Unfair Claims Settlement Practices Act, without empowering state regulatory authorities to resolve individual claims and without infringing upon proper functions of the judiciary, attempts to define unfair insurance claims practices. It also gives state regulatory authorities a range of sanctions—fines, injunctions, and rehabilitations—for use in those cases where the unfair practices are systematically present. The New York Insurance Department believed that the existence of these sanctions would work to deter most companies from engaging in unfair claims practices without the state insurance department having to intervene on behalf of the public.[20]

Provisions of the Act The NAIC Model Act borrows most of the language of the New York statute and includes fourteen sections. The conduct described in any of these provisions constitutes an unfair claims practice:

1. Misrepresenting pertinent facts or insurance policy provisions relating to coverages at issue;
2. Failing to acknowledge and act reasonably promptly upon communications with respect to claims arising under insurance policies;
3. Failing to adopt and implement reasonable standards for the prompt investigation of claims;
4. Refusing to pay claims without conducting a reasonable investigation based upon all available information;
5. Failing to affirm or deny coverage of claims within a reasonable time after proof of loss statements have been completed;
6. Not attempting in good faith to effectuate prompt, fair, and equitable settlements of claims in which liability has become reasonably clear;
7. Compelling insureds to institute litigation to recover amounts due under an insurance policy by offering substantially less than the amounts ultimately recovered in actions by such insureds;
8. Attempting to settle a claim for less than the amount to which a reasonable man would have believed he was entitled by reference to written or principal advertising material accompanying or made part of an application;
9. Attempting to settle claims on the basis of an application which was altered without notice to or knowledge of insureds;
10. Making claims payments to insureds or beneficiaries not accompanied by statements setting forth the coverage under which the payments are being made;
11. Making known to insureds or claimants a policy of appealing from arbitration awards in favor of insureds or claimants for the purpose of compelling them to accept settlements or compromises less than the amount awarded in arbitration;
12. Delaying the investigation or payment of claims by requiring an insured, claimant, or the physician of either to submit a preliminary claim report and then requiring the subsequent

submission of formal proof of loss forms, both of which submissions contain substantially the same information;

13. Failing to promptly settle claims where liability has become reasonably clear under one portion of the insurance policy coverage, in order to influence settlements under other portions of the insurance policy coverage; and

14. Failing to provide promptly a reasonable explanation of the basis relied on in the insurance policy in relation to the facts or applicable law for denial of a claim or for the offer of a compromise settlement.

Significance of the Act to You It would be advisable for you to memorize the substance of these fourteen points, since they have a definite bearing on your future success as a claims adjuster. It is likely that all states will adopt some version of the Model Act.

A majority of the states have the Model Act provisions, and a substantial number of additional states have most of the Act in effect. Some states include provisions that add to the responsibilities of claims personnel. In other states, a search of the statutes will not give you much information about unfair claims practices. In those states, it is quite possible that an "enabling" act of the legislature has given the state insurance department the necessary authority to promulgate rules and regulations pertaining to unfair claims practices. Several of the states have done this, and the state insurance department has incorporated the NAIC Model Act in the state department's rules and regulations. These have the same force and effect as if they were written into the state law.

If you wish to be successful and stay out of trouble in claims handling, you must be familiar with your state statutes, insurance department rules and regulations, and court interpretations of the foregoing. You must also realize that laws and rules *can and do change* rapidly in many cases. You must be alert to change.

In comparing the requirements of your state law with the NAIC Model Act, you may discover that there are a number of variations between your state's requirements and those of the Model Act. For example, your state's law may include only a portion of the provisions in the Model Act, or they may be paraphrased in such a way that they combine sections. In other cases, there will be entirely different requirements added to the Model Act.

Requirements of Record Keeping In addition, most of the Acts and the administrative rules and regulations require insurers to keep records of all complaints including those regarding claims. A typical statute declares the following to be an unfair claims settlement practice:

Failing of any insurer to maintain a complete record of all of the complaints which it has received since the date of its last examination. This record shall indicate the total number of complaints, their classification by line of insurance, the nature of each complaint, the disposition of these complaints, and the time it took to process each complaint. For purposes of this paragraph, "complaint" shall mean any written communication primarily expressing a grievance.

Some insurance department rules and regulations can be so demanding that they impose serious problems for an individual adjuster. For example, one state's rules provide:

If the Department of Insurance observes that an insurer's claims settlement practices are not meeting the standards established by statute or by this subchapter, the Department may require such insurer to file periodic reports. Depending on the nature and extent of an insurer's deviations from such standards and with due consideration of the insurer's data capabilities, the Commissioner in his discretion may require the report to include some or all of the statistics listed below:
1. The total number of claims submitted;
2. The original amount claimed;
3. The classification by line of insurance of each individual claim;
4. The total number of claims denied;
5. The total number of claims paid;
6. The total number of claims compromised;
7. The amount of each settlement;
8. The total number of claims for which lawsuits are instituted against the insurer, the reason for the lawsuit, and the amount of the final ajudication; and
9. An individual listing showing the disposition and other information for each claim.

Significance of Record-Keeping Requirement to You All of the record-keeping requirements that now confront insurance companies mean that there will be written reports of all complaints. Most likely the adjuster involved will also be identified; in the event that a lawsuit or a complaint from the state insurance department results, you will definitely be involved. This has rather serious ramifications for the adjuster, because it puts you in the spotlight. Consequently, you should strive to act responsibly, documenting and controlling your file to demonstrate conscientious, prudent, and good-faith handling.

In an earlier chapter, it was pointed out that a number of states are revising the tort law regarding "joint and several" liability. You will also recall from a discussion in an earlier chapter that there are legislative attempts to avoid the so-called "Deep Pocket" phenomenon. Big corporations, including insurance companies, have always been prime targets for litigation. Since the plaintiffs have always known that these big corporations have a great deal of assets, or "Deep Pockets," these big companies have been excellent defendants for litigation.

Since the old tort doctrine of joint and several liability makes it possible for a plaintiff to choose to sue all or any one of the individuals responsible for alleged damages and collect the total amount from any of the parties responsible, it has been natural for attorneys to proceed primarily or exclusively against the big corporation. Now that states are beginning to enact legislation that modifies the doctrine, the result will be that each individual defendant will be responsible for only that person's or corporation's percentage of fault for noneconomic damages such as pain and suffering.

Because of these changes, attorneys are likely to try more energetically to recover damages from all of the parties responsible for a given loss. Thus, if you and your insurance company employer are sued for damages resulting from unfair claims practices, bad faith, and so on, it is quite likely that you may end up being liable for part of a judgment in the event that the plaintiff prevails in a lawsuit. This will mean that your employer will have to carry considerable liability insurance on you, or you will personally have to provide adequate professional liability coverage to cover your performance.

Variation in Unfair Claims Statutes

Some states have brief unfair claims statutes. For example, states may have only a few provisions in their statutes, but they may be couched in such general terms that they cover a host of alleged evils. One state has only a three-part Act. Another covers only five points of the Model Act.

A number of states, however, have defined other acts as "unfair claims practices," and these promise to complicate the lives of all claims adjusters. Some of these acts are:

1. Directly advising a claimant not to obtain the services of an attorney.
2. Misleading a claimant as to the applicable statute of limitations.
3. Requiring an insured or claimant to submit to any polygraph test concerning a claim.
4. Using as a basis for cash settlement with a first-party automobile insurance claimant an amount which is less than the amount which the insurer would be charged if repairs were made unless such amount is agreed to by the insured or provided for by the insurance policy.
5. Engaging in activity which results in a disproportionate number of meritorious complaints against the insurer received by the Insurance Department.

6. Engaging in activity which results in a disproportionate number of lawsuits to be filed by the claimants against the insurer or its insureds.

7. If a claim is denied, and the claimant objects, failing to notify the claimant that he or she may have the matter reviewed by the state insurance department and providing the claimant with the address and telephone number of the department.

8. Refusing payment of a third-party claim solely on the basis of an insured's request to do so without making an independent evaluation of the insured's liability based upon all available information.

9. Refusing payment of a third-party claim solely on the basis of an insured's request to do so unless:

   a. the insured claims sovereign, eleemosynary, diplomatic, military service, or other immunity from suit or liability with respect to such claim; or

   b. the insured is granted the right under the policy of insurance to consent to settlement of claims.

10. Requiring an insured or a third-party claimant to use a drive-in claim service operated by the insurer. The voluntary utilization of a drive-in claim service shall not prejudice the right of either party to obtain independent appraisals and negotiate settlement on the basis of such appraisals.

11. If the insurer makes a deduction for the salvage value of a "total loss" vehicle retained by the claimant, failing to furnish the claimant with the name and address of the salvage dealer who will purchase the salvage for the amount deducted, if so requested by the claimant.

12. Requiring a claimant to obtain more than two estimates of property damage and failing to bear the cost of acquiring such additional estimates.

13. Withholding the entire amount of a loss or claims payment because the insured owes premiums or other monies in an amount less than the loss or claims payment.

14. Deducting from a loss or claims payment made under one policy those premiums owed by the insured on another policy, unless the insured consents.

15. Requiring an insured to sign a release that extends beyond the subject matter that gave rise to the claims payment.

16. Denying a claim for failure of a claimant to submit to a physical examination or for failure of the claimant to exhibit the property which is the subject of the claim without proof of demand by such insurer in the form of a written request and an unfounded refusal by a claimant to do so.

17. Failing to pay a claim where fraud or arson are suspected unless the insurer has specific evidence, including but not limited to reports from law enforcement agencies, sworn statements, documentary evidence, or real evidence that would reasonably provide probable cause to believe that the first-party claimant or third-party claimant has fraudulently caused or contributed to the loss by arson or any other unlawful or fraudulent means.

18. Failing to settle first-party claims on the basis that responsibility for payment should be assumed by others except as may otherwise be provided by policy provisions.

19. Failing to carry and exhibit upon request a license card in order to identify the adjuster's authority.

20. Requiring that third-party claimants make claims under their own policies solely to avoid paying claims under the adjusting insurer's insurance policy or insurance contract.

21. Requiring a claimant to travel unreasonably either to inspect a replacement automobile, to obtain a repair estimate, or to have the automobile repaired at a specific repair shop.

22. If the insured's motor vehicle is repaired at the repair shop recommended by the insurer, for a sum estimated by the insurer as the reasonable cost to repair the vehicle, the insurer:
    a. shall select a repair shop that issues written guarantees that any work performed in repairing damaged motor vehicles meets generally accepted standards for safe and proper repairs;
    b. shall cause the damaged vehicle to be restored to its condition prior to the loss, at no additional cost to the insured and within a reasonable time, if the repair shop it recommended does not repair the damaged motor vehicle in accordance with generally accepted standards for safe and proper repair.

23. Issuing checks or drafts in partial settlement of a loss or a claim under a specified coverage which contains language which purports to release the insurer or its insured from total liability.

24. Unfairly discriminating against claimants because they are represented by a public adjuster.

25. Failing to expeditiously honor drafts given in settlement of claims.

26. Failing to adopt and implement reasonable standards for the processing and payment of claims once the obligation to pay has been established.

27. Withholding any portion of any benefit payable as a result of a claim on the basis that the sum withheld is an adjustment or

correction or an overpayment made on a prior claim arising under the same policy unless:

    a. the company has within its files clear, documented evidence of an overpayment and written authorization from the insured permitting such withholding procedure or

    b. the company has within its files clear, documented evidence of the following:

       i. the overpayment was clearly erroneous under the provisions of the policy. If the overpayment is the subject of reasonable dispute as to the facts, this procedure may not be used.

      ii. The error which resulted in the payment is not a mistake of law.

     iii. The company notifies the insured within six (6) months of the date of the error, except that in instances of error prompted by representations or nondisclosures of claimants or third parties, the company notifies the insured within fifteen working days after the date that clear, documented evidence of discovery of such error is included in its file.

     iv. Such notice states clearly the nature of the error and the amount of the overpayment.

28. Any notice rejecting any element of a claim involving personal property insurance shall contain the identity and the claims processing address of the insurer, the insured's policy number, the claim number, and the following statement prominently set out:

> Should you wish to take this matter up with the New York State Insurance Department, you may write or visit a consumer services bureau, New York State Insurance Department. . . . (address follows)

There are many other standards that are established under state statutes and insurance department administrative rules and regulations for proper claims handling. A considerable number of these establish specific time limitations for performing various claims procedures—time limits on beginning an investigation of any claim filed by a claimant or by a claimant's authorized representative; time limits on payment of claims or denial of claims; and various time limits regarding communications to insureds or third-party claimants.

It is important for you as a person involved in handling insurance claims to realize that virtually none of these restrictions or rules of conduct applied to claims adjusters until 1970. It is a new world out there for claims adjusters. It is a particularly disturbing and distressing world for experienced claims personnel who have been in the business for many years. It is a dangerous world for those of you who are just beginning to enter the business. You must know the dangers.

A thorough familiarity with the "Do's" and "Don'ts" of claims handling is essential. Study the laws and rules and regulations in those states where you will be involved. Many adjusters, such as independent adjusters, operate in virtually any state and are assigned to handle claims wherever there is a major disaster. They are faced with a jungle of laws, rules, and regulations. Whether you operate in one state or many, you must be particularly careful to observe the cardinal requirements of "aggressive good faith," while acting responsibly in furtherance of your employer's or client's legitimate business interests:

1. The "Immediate Contact Rule"
2. Timely and continual communication
3. Diligence
4. Honesty
5. Fairness
6. Reasonableness

"General Business Practice"—Standard Language

Most of the states that have enacted Unfair Claims Settlement Practices Statutes have incorporated standard language that would seem to foreclose private rights of action under their statute.[21] You may recall from your reading of the New York Statute earlier in the chapter that the law provides that certain acts are illegal if "performed with such frequency as to indicate a *general business practice*" (emphasis added). Most of the states have followed this language.

Other states have enacted statutes with slight variations of the standard language. For example, Alaska's statute reads, "... with such frequency as to indicate a practice." Florida applies the standard language only on punitive damages and does not require a general business practice of the unfair claims settlement practice spelled out in its act. Three states—Missouri, Pennsylvania, and Vermont—have language in their statutes that refers to a "business practice," merely omitting "general" from the language. Similar variations exist in other states.

With the statutory requirement of "a general business practice," a "persistent tendency," or other such language, one would be disposed to conclude that more than one isolated incident would be required to show violation of the statute. Indeed, the record-keeping requirements of the various statutes were designed to accumulate the information regarding claims handling that would show whether a "general practice" existed in the claims practices of an individual insurer.

Notwithstanding the language of the various statutes, some courts have held that a single violation knowingly committed is a sufficient basis for action under the statutes.[22] Since Florida does not require "a general business practice," an isolated case of improper claims handling would appear to give rise to a cause of action against the insurance company and its errant claims adjuster.

It would be unwise for an insurer or an individual adjuster to rely on the fact that only one offense may have been committed under the statutes. Courts have a tendency to look at the gravity of the offense, and, particularly in those situations where a court or jury is appalled by the conduct in question, notwithstanding the language of the statute, the courts may rule that a single offense satisfies the statute—as they have in California.

The safest course of conduct that can be followed by an insurer and its claims adjusters is to assume that every mistake or transgression of the state statutes may ultimately lead to trouble. Whatever the case, a party that believes he or she has been wronged by an insurer or an adjuster may bring a lawsuit. Thereafter, an inquiry will be made into the records of the company to determine whether a "general business practice" has been established. The fact that there is a single, isolated incident, therefore, will not keep the insurance company and the adjuster out of court.

The Usual Complaint

Examination of the many cases that have reached the courts concerning Unfair Claims Settlement Practices Acts suggests that a large number of the cases arise because of one major complaint. This is based upon the sixth subdivision of Section 9: "(6) not attempting in good faith to effectuate prompt, fair and equitable settlements of claims in which liability has become reasonably clear."

The history of "bad faith" litigation has made it easier for attorneys to proceed on this particular offense, since there is a substantial body of law relating to bad faith cases. In some cases, of course, it is merely necessary to show that an insurer and adjuster have been negligent, since in some jurisdictions negligence and bad faith seem to be synonymous.

This particular section of the Unfair Claims Settlement Practices Act is sort of a catch-all section that covers all of the cardinal points of "aggressive good faith" mentioned before.

This section can cover maliciousness and other misconduct on the part of the adjuster, but can also cover simple errors of judgment and often will include a great deal of conduct which is entirely proper.

For example, many of the cases arise out of the complaint that an insurance company failed to settle a claim within the policy limits. The decision to refuse to make settlement and to litigate the case can be based upon the most informed legal judgment and outstanding evidential file prepared by the claims adjuster. However, the old truism that "there is no case so good that it can't be lost and no case so bad that it can't be won" applies. Thus, a company may be performing the claims-handling function through its claims adjusters in the most proper and competent manner, and a capricious, arbitrary jury that does not happen to like insurance companies, may still award exorbitant verdicts for plaintiffs bringing suit against the insurers and their adjusters.

Other cases have come about because of alleged failure on the part of the insurer and the adjuster to adopt and implement reasonable standards for the prompt investigation of claims; refusing to pay claims without conducting a reasonable investigation based upon all available information; and failing to affirm or deny coverage of claims within a reasonable time after proof of loss statements have been completed. The other provisions of the Act have also brought forth many lawsuits. Most cases result because of delay and lack of communications.

Again, in order to protect yourself against a possible claim under the statutes, you should be absolutely familiar with your own state statutes and insurance department rules and regulations. Further, you should be familiar with the variations in statutes that exist in other states, because those alleged rules of misconduct may be applied in your particular situation, notwithstanding the provisions of your own state's law, given the broad decisions of judges and the capricious and arbitrary verdicts of juries that sometimes crop up in these cases.

SANCTIONS CREATED UNDER THE NEW LAWS

The new unfair claims settlement practices statutes have created new sanctions that can be imposed against insurance adjusters and their employers. Included in those sanctions are new powers that have been given to state insurance departments, expanding their already-existing powers over insurers and specifically addressing the subject of unfair claims practices.

In addition, a number of states provide direct rights of action to insureds, providing extra-contractual rights of action for third-party claimants under the new statutes.

Insurance Departments—New Powers Needed

Prior to the enactment of the new statutes, state insurance

departments had authority generally to police the activities of insurance practitioners, including claims adjusters. For example, in some states, claims adjusters had to be licensed. Licenses are a privilege. They are subject to revocation or suspension. Some state insurance departments have exercised the power of revocation or suspension, particularly in the case of life insurance agents. However, the power has been utilized infrequently, if ever, in the case of claims adjusters.

Individual state insurance departments have expressed a frustration and impotency in dealing with abuses in the handling of insurance claims. The experience of the states of New York, New Jersey, Minnesota, and Massachusetts is illustrative. There was strong belief on the part of the departments that they required additional authority over the area of insurance claims handling.

The New York Experience   Prior to the enactment of the New York Unfair Claims Statute, the State Insurance Department in its annual report gave a statement in support of the new law. The statement declared that under the then presently existing law, an insurance company's obligation to deal fairly with claimants and policy holders in the settlement of claims—and indeed, in simple obligations to pay claims at all—was solely a matter of private contract law. No provision of the law required an insurance company to pay claims. Nor did the law give any state agency other than the courts any power to determine contractual claim disputes. As a result, if an insurance company unfairly refused to pay a claim, the consumer was relegated to the courts, with the inherent problems of delay and expense.

The report claimed that general courses of conduct or general business practices cannot be effectively dealt with by individual litigants in the courts. It stated:

> [If] These general business practices are to be affected directly—rather than only indirectly through the discipline of individual cases—this can best and most profitably be by an administrative agency which exercises a continuing surveillance over the licensees and the practices in question.[23]

The New York Department reported that wide variations in claims settlement practices existed among insurers, and in many cases, an investigation into a complaint revealed that the insurance company was correct in its dealing with the consumer, or the company at least had a possible defense which it was entitled to assert in court. The Department concluded that in many cases the insurer's failure, if there was a failure, was that of lack of communication rather than a failure in fair dealing.

In other cases, the insurer's initial resistance or delay evaporated when a complaint was made to the Department, and the matter was then promptly settled. Finally, there were some cases where the Department's lack of power to compel fair settlements meant that a recalcitrant insurer could persist indefinitely in an unreasonable position.

But even if every complaint made to the Department was quickly and satisfactorily resolved, consumers still would not be adequately protected by the then prevailing system. That was so because an insurance company's initial delay was bad in itself, and there were undoubtedly more claimants receiving unsatisfactory treatment from insurers who did not, for one reason or another, make a complaint to the Department.[24]

The New Jersey Experience   The New Jersey Department of Insurance expressed similar frustration in its inability to handle complaints regarding insurance claims-handling practices. Supporting its new unfair claims statute, the Department declared:

> Upon the single, central act of making a claim and having it paid rests the whole rationale for the legitimacy of insurance. If this objective is not achieved, then nothing is achieved; and we believe that the conditions necessary for its achievement are deserving of more systematic and explicit consideration than they have received in the past.[25]

The Department reported that it had frequently observed examples of the unfair practices that the New Jersey regulations were intended to eliminate, such as some companies engaging in incompetent and deliberate exploitative handling of their customers' claims.

In addition, it was observed that there were pressures that can at times make even the best-intentioned companies more likely to adopt excessively restrictive claims practices. For example, in cyclical periods, poor underwriting results can quickly affect a company's claims practices. Even in the best of times, the absence of specific guidelines for achieving the goals set forth in generally formulated statutory standards for the claims settlement can and do lead to varied and contradictory interpretations of what the law requires.

The Department felt powerless when it complained about the appropriateness of a particular claims practice, particularly when an insurer defended on the basis that there was no existing specific rule interpreting the statutory requirements. In addition, the Department cited an opinion of more than one hundred pages by an administrative law judge who found that an insurer had violated the Unfair Trade

Practices Statute, but the judge was troubled by the absence of definitive rules implementing this statutory standard.

When New Jersey's Department described the complaints it had received from third parties, insurance companies complained that their conduct towards third-party claimants was entirely consistent with contract law. The insurer spokesmen declared that they had contractual responsibility only to their insureds rather than to third-party claimants. In response, the Department stated that the state legislature and the courts have increasingly recognized the general social responsibility to be discharged through the liability insurance mechanism and that third-party claimants are entitled to be treated with courtesy and fairness.[26]

The Minnesota Experience Prior to 1973, Minnesota had neither legislative nor administrative guidelines setting forth standards of conduct for insurance companies in the settlement of a claim. Further, the Attorney General could not take action against any insurance company for violation of consumer statutes.

As recently as 1979, the State Supreme Court stated that bad faith in the breach of an insurance contract did not convert a contract action into a tort. The state legislature in 1973 enacted legislation that gave the Commissioner of Insurance the power to establish regulations that would insure the prompt, fair, and honest processing of claims and complaints; however, rules and regulations were never established.

By 1984, the Minnesota Department of Commerce, the insurance regulatory agency, annually received approximately 6,000 complaints regarding the conduct of insurance carriers in the negotiation and settlement of claims. These complaints related to all types of insurance—health, accident, life, or casualty—and involved first-party insureds, third-party claimants, public and captive adjusters, and agents. Up to that time the Department of Commerce had never taken disciplinary action against an insurance company for any unfair, deceptive, or fraudulent conduct during the claims process. The failure to take action was caused in part by the lack of legislative authority and the lack of administrative guidelines.

Minnesota's unfair claims statute was passed primarily at the urging of insurance agents throughout the state who had repeatedly found it increasingly difficult to negotiate claims between their clients and their companies. The act is designed to give both the department and the citizen, both insureds and third-party claimants, the tools with which to assure the prompt, fair, and equitable resolution of claims.[27]

The Massachusetts Experience Chapter 93A of the Massachusetts General Laws Annotated prohibits "unfair or deceptive acts or practices in the conduct of any trade or commerce." This is the state's

Unfair Trade Practices Act. Under the Massachusetts law the Attorney General may investigate and bring an action for violation of this statute.

The Massachusetts courts, however, have been critical of the ability of both the Attorney General and the state Commissioner of Insurance to protect the public. The courts state:

> The Attorney General had been unable effectively to obtain relief for individual consumers because of the tremendous volume of complaints his office received after enactment of c.93A.[28]

In the case of the Commissioner of Insurance of the state, a court declared:

> Like the Attorney General, the Commissioner of Insurance has limited resources with which to vindicate individuals' wrongs, so he too must focus his attention on insurance practices he finds most deleterious to the public interest, leaving small but valid claims unattended.[29]

Despite this declared impotency of the Attorney General's Office and that of the State Department of Insurance, the Massachusetts courts have consistently applied the doctrines of primary jurisdiction and the exhaustion of administrative remedies. In other words, a person must exhaust the possibilities of receiving relief from the administrative agencies before turning to the courts for relief.[30]

New Powers of Insurance Departments   The new statutes give the state insurance departments a broad range of new sanctions that can be applied against insurance companies and claims adjusters. These apply in the relationship with the insured and in many states with the third-party claimant. Even in states where a direct cause of action is not provided by law for the third-party claimant, the state insurance department has broad authority over the conduct of adjusters and the way they treat third-party claimants.

The New York Insurance Department's regulations are illustrative of the duties you owe to third-party claimants. For example, for third-party property damage claims arising under motor vehicle liability insurance contracts, there are strict rules regarding your obligation to acknowledge the receipt of notice of claim and either make a timely payment or a denial of claim, setting forth the reasons. Some states, such as New York, also prescribe the content of letters that must be sent to insureds, as well as setting standards which must be met in providing information on the denial of claims to either insureds or third-party claimants.

In addition to the existing rights of license suspension and revocation, the new laws give the insurance departments a wide range of sanctions, such as fines, injunctions, and rehabilitation procedures for those who violate these statutes or departmental rules and regulations. Further, interest on overdue claims payments, attorneys' fees, and court costs can be assessed against those who violate the law.

Insureds' Rights of Action

Although there are several states that prohibit private rights of action based on their state statutes or administrative rules and regulations, there are at least twenty other states that provide a direct private cause of action for insureds under the new Unfair Claims Settlement Practice Statutes or under existing Unfair Trade Practice Statutes. Courts and legislatures, as well as the insurance departments themselves, are moving more and more toward allowing private rights of action, particularly in the case of insureds. More and more criticism is being directed toward giving insurance departments exclusivity of remedy under the new statutes and department rules and regulations. Illustrative of this philosophy favoring insureds is a federal court case severely criticizing the argument that the new body of unfair claims statutes provides exclusivity of remedy in the state insurance departments, barring a private right of action by an insured. The federal court declared that administrative exclusivity of remedy offers:

> Little solace to an insured who has to depend on the cumbersome investigative and enforcement mechanism explicitly provided by the Code. The Code does not even provide a penalty for engaging in an unlawful practice until the Commissioner conducts an investigation, determines there is reason to believe a violation has occurred, holds a hearing, issues a cease and desist order, and then proves to the court that the offender has violated the cease and desist order.[31]

Third-Party Rights of Action

An increasing number of states are providing direct rights of action for third parties, an extra-contractual right of action based on state statute or departmental rules and regulations. One of the early cases providing third-party rights of action was the Royal Globe Insurance Company Case, in which the California Supreme Court ruled that the state legislature intended to permit third parties to sue and recover under the state Unfair Claims Settlement Practices Act.[32] Some of the other states that have joined California include Connecticut, Florida, Montana, West Virginia, and Minnesota.

The trend toward permitting third parties to have an extra-contractual right of action under the new statutes seems to be a matter of public policy designed "to gain prompt compensation of injured persons, encourage settlements, and discourage litigation. Insurers may not sit back and relax simply because court congestion shields them for a time."[33]

Whether it is desirable or in the public interest to exclude private rights of action under the Unfair Claims Settlement Practices legislation is subject to debate. It is understandable that some state insurance departments argue for primary jurisdiction and for the doctrine of exhaustion of administrative remedies, if not outright exclusivity of remedy. This is the course taken by a handful of states.

Nevertheless, there is a strong sentiment in other states in the form of statutes, court decisions, and administrative rules and regulations against giving the state insurance department sole enforcement authority and foreclosing private rights of action. The creation of private causes of action under the Unfair Claims Settlement Laws demonstrates a manifestation of a public mood—an unsympathetic and hostile impatience with insurance companies and some expression of no confidence and/or ignorance of the functions of state insurance departments.

CONCLUSIONS

Now that you have read this far, it must be abundantly clear to you that the task of handling insurance claims in a proper manner is fraught with a great deal of potential trouble and difficulty. It is worth repeating that the Unfair Claims Practices Rules specified in your own state must be completely understood by you. In addition, you should have a general understanding of the statutory provisions and rules and regulations described in this chapter, as well as those that apply in other states, because you never know when your own state courts may decide to apply those standards as a broadening of the interpretation of your state's statutes.

Never before has the job of the insurance claims adjuster been so demanding in terms of human relations. Everyone, whether insured or third-party claimant, must be treated with the utmost courtesy and consideration.

No matter how tired you may be on a given day, and no matter how large your case load happens to be, you cannot for a moment forget that you have an absolute responsibility to handle all claims in a prompt and reasonable manner. This involves immediate and continual communication with the other party and demands the utmost of fairness, courtesy, and consideration. To engage in any other type of conduct subjects you to potential liability, not only because of sanctions that may be imposed by your state insurance department, but because you also face the likelihood that you may be directly sued by the insured, the third-party claimant, or both.

The only solution to avoiding trouble is to practice "aggressive good faith." In all your dealings with the public, you must focus on human relations. Try to forget the fact that you are an "insurance claims adjuster." Under today's legal climate and societal expectations, you are a "people adjuster," not a claims adjuster.

Particularly those who handle claims by telephone should "put a smile in your voice." Work hard to develop a telephone personality that reflects caring, compassion, concern, consideration, and courtesy—the five "C's" of good human relations in communication.

Stir some warmth into your voice and the handling of your claims files. Despite what you perceive to be an inordinate case load, keep your files "warm," by making frequent contact with insureds and third-party claimants. There is nothing that will send an insured or a claimant to an attorney faster than seeming to ignore the needs of the insured or the claimant.

Spokespersons for the American Trial Lawyers Association state that they receive much of their business from people whose claims have been ignored.[34] Keeping your files active by periodic contact with insureds and claimants can keep you out of court.

Chapter Notes

1. 9 Wheaton 1.
2. Robert I. Mehr and Emerson Cammack, *Principles of Insurance* (Homewood, IL: Richard D. Irwin, Inc., 1976), p. 662.
3. 8 Wall 183 (1869) *Paul v. Virginia* set the pattern for insurance regulation for seventy-five years.
4. *Railway v. Van Husen*, 95 U.S. 465 (1872); *Pensacola Tel. Co. v. Western Union*, 96 U. S. 1 (1877).
5. *United States v. South-Eastern Underwriters Association et al.*, 322 U. S. 533 (1944).
6. The McCarran-Ferguson Act has come under increasing attack in recent years because of the alleged failure of some state insurance departments to adequately regulate the business of insurance. Attempts have been made to repeal the Act. If the Act is repealed, the industry will be faced with rather extensive federal regulation.
7. The Florida statute outlawing commission rebates to buyers was declared unconstitutional in 1986.
8. *Amalgamated Utility Workers v. Consolidated Edison Co. of New York*, 309 U. S. 261, 268, 60 S. Ct. 561, 84 L. ed. 738 (1940)(dictum); *Holloway v. Bristol-Meyers Corp.*, 485 Fed. 2d 986 (D.C. Cir. 1973); *United States v. St. Regis Paper Co.*, 355 Fed. 2d 688, 693 (2d Cir. 1966)(dictum); *New Jersey Wood Finishing Co. v. Minnesota Mining and Manufacturing Co.*, 332 F. 2d 346, 352 (3d Cir. 1964)(dictum), aff'd. 381 U. S. 311, 85 S. Ct. 1473, 14 L. ed. 2d 405 (1965); *Holloway v. Bristol-Meyers Corp.*, 327 F. Supp. 17 (D.D.C. 1971); *LaSalle Street Press, Inc. v. McCormick and Henderson Inc.*, 293 F. Supp. 1004 (N. D. Ill. 1968); *Smith-Victor Corp. v. Sylvania Electric Products, Inc.*, 242 F. Supp. 302 (N. D. Ill. 1965); *L'Aiglon Apparel, Inc. v. Lana Lobell, Inc.*, 118 F. Supp. 251 (E.D. Pa. 1953); *Samson Crane Company v. Union National Sales, Inc.* 87 F. Supp. 218, 221 (D. Mass. 1949), aff'd. 180 F. 2d 896 (1st Cir. 1950); *National Fruit Product Co. v. Dwinell-Wright Co.*, 47 F. Supp. 499 (D. Mass. 1942); *Atlanta Brick Co. v. O'Neal*, 44 F. Supp. 39 (E.D. Tex. 1942); *Skelton v. General Motors*, 500 F. Supp. 1181 (N. D. Ill. 1980), citing *Holloway v. Bristol-Meyers Corp.*, 485 F. 2d 986 (D. C. Cir. 1973).
9. *French Market Plaza Corp. v. Sequoia Insurance Co.*, 480 F. Supp. 821 at 826 (1979 La.), referring to Section 22:1213, Louisiana Revised Statutes Annotated.
10. Maine Revised Statutes Annotated, see Title 5, Chapter 10, Sections 207 and 213.
11. *Bartner v. Carter*, 405 A. 2d 194 (1979), ruling that a consumer's action under Section 213 "was not for damages generally but was for restitution."
12. Vernon's Civil Statutes of the State of Texas Annot., Article 21.21 (16) 1985 amendment.

13. See for example, *Mayo v. John Hancock Mutual Life Insurance*, 699 S.W. 2d 724 (Texas, App. 5 Dist. 1985).

14. *Traveler's Health Assn. v. FTC*, 362 U. S. 293 (1960), reversing 262 F.2d 241 (1959). The decision applied only to the state of Nebraska, but the legal ruling was extended to all other states by *Traveler's Health Assn. v. FTC*, 298 F. 2d 820 (8th Cir., 1962).

15. *U. S. vs. Chicago Title and Trust Company et al.*, 242 F. Supp. 56 (N.D. Ill., 1965); *U. S. v. Investors Diversified Services*, 297 CCH Trade Cases 116, Section 69, 574 (1954); *U. S. v. New Orleans Insurance Exchange*, 148 F. Supp. 915, aff'd., per curiam, 355 U. S. 22 (1957).

16. *S.E.C. v. Variable Annuity Life Insurance Company of America et al.*, 359 U. S. 65 (1959).

17. *Prudential Insurance Company of America v. S.E.C.*, 326 F. 2d 383 (1964).

18. Willis Park Rokes, *Human Relations in Handling Insurance Claims* (Homewood, IL: Richard D. Irwin, Inc., 1967), p. 250 and 1981 edition, p. 342.

19. Section 40-d Insurance Law, added L. 1970, c. 296, Section 1, amended L. 1981, c. 711, Section 4.

20. Superintendent of Insurance, State of New York 111th Annual Report, p. 37

21. Willis Park Rokes, "Legislative Intent Under the State Unfair Claims Settlement Practices Statute—Are Private Rights of Action Foreclosed?" *The Journal of Insurance Regulation* (June 1984), p. 436.

22. *Royal Globe Insurance Company v. Superior Court of Butte County*, 592 P. 2d 329 at 336 (1979, Cal.); and see, *Jackson v. State Farm Mutual Automobile Insurance Co.*, 196 Cal. Rptr. 494 (1983).

23. *Id.*, pp. 37-38.

24. *Id.*, p. 38.

25. New Jersey State Insurance Department, "A Report on the Unfair Claims Settlement Practices Regulation" (N.J.A.C. 11:2-17), p. 2.

26. *Id.*, pp. 2-4.

27. Michael A. Hatch, " 'Unfair Claims Practices Act' Creates Positive Cause of Action," *Minnesota Trial Lawyer* (Special Edition, 1984), pp. 4-7. The article was written by the Commissioner of the Minnesota Department of Commerce.

28. *Slaney v. Westwood Auto, Inc.*, 366 Mass. 688, 698-699, 322 N.E.2d 768 (1975).

29. *Dodd v. Commercial Union Insurance Co.*, 365 N.E.2d 802 at 805 (Mass. 1977).

30. *Gordon v. Hardware Mut. Cas. Co.*, 361 Mass. 582, 588, 281 N.E.2d 573 (1972).

31. *French Market Plaza Corp. v. Sequoia Insurance Co.*, 480 F. Supp. 821 at 825 (La. 1979).

32. *Royal Globe Insurance Co. v. Superior Court of Butte County*, 153 Cal. Rptr. 842, 592 P.2d 329 (1979).

33. *Avila v. Traveler's Insurance Companies*, 481 F.Supp. 431 (Cal. 1979).

34. Willis Park Rokes, *Human Relations In Handling Insurance Claims* (Homewood, IL: Richard D. Irwin, Inc. 1981), pp. 349-350.

CHAPTER 5

Aggressive Good Faith

Good faith is the antithesis, or exact opposite, of bad faith; and bad faith and its consequence are the subject of the preceding chapters. John H. Holmes, an Oregon attorney, uses the term "aggressive good faith" to signify the type of behavior which *must* be adopted by today's claims adjusters.[1]

Bad faith conduct in the handling of insurance claims spawned the evolution of "bad faith" litigation. First, we had some breach of contract cases. Judges and juries awarded plaintiffs damages for an insurer's breach of the implied covenant of good faith and fair dealing. This was a good faith requirement to perform faithfully the fiduciary responsibilities owed to the insured by the insurer by virtue of the insurance policy or contract.

As the public, as evidenced by jury verdicts and judges' awards, expressed more outrage at insurers' (and their adjusters') bad faith conduct, the law recognized that breach of the implied contractual warranty of good faith and fair dealing could also be a tort wrong. That conduct carried the elements of unconscionability, recklessness, gross negligence, and willful misconduct, and conveyed the wrongdoers' "furtive design or some motive of ill will." Insincerity, dishonesty, disloyalty, duplicity, deceitful conduct, fraud, or concealment became important aspects of the bad faith tort.

A corollary development of the bad faith litigation was the transformation of the bad faith tort into a quasi-criminal matter, justifying the punishment of the offending insurer by awarding the plaintiff punitive or exemplary damages. And we have seen that enormous jury verdicts were awarded as punitive damages to punish insurers believed to be errant in their claims handling behavior.

Punitive damages are designed to provide for the promotion of justice and to provide an extraordinary remedy for the victim of the wrongdoing. Such damages may also serve to deter others from committing the same type of conduct. As discussed in Chapter 3, punitive damages have provided a partial remedy for the defect in American civil procedure where compensatory damages awarded are inadequate or where they are denied. For example, punitive damages serve as compensation where conduct has been particularly deplorable but there has been absence of actual damages.

To summarize, punitive damages serve the following objectives:

1. To punish;
2. To promote justice;
3. To deter others from onerous or bad conduct; and
4. To provide for a deficiency in compensatory damages.

Four theories justifying the award of punitive damages have been discussed in some detail by Professor John D. Long[2]

As claims handling complaints proliferated, state insurance departments, insurance agents, and the insuring public complained to their legislators. Consumer organizations added their voices to the clamor for reform. The Consumers Union organization in its *Consumer Reports* periodically afforded reports of the volume of public complaints against individual insurance companies. Individual critics attacked the industry on a variety of complaints—claims handling, marketing practices (life insurance and other lines), advertising, inadequate state regulation, insolvency and mismanagement of insurers, and a host of other alleged inadequacies.

Federal agencies were among the critics. The Federal Trade Commission was joined by a host of other critics. Included among these were the Chairman of the Anti-trust and Monopoly Subcommittee of the U.S. Senate Judiciary Committee, academicians, and others.

Ultimately, the invevitable occurred. The states enacted the Unfair Claims Settlement Practices statutes, described in Chapter 4. They include the fourteen unfair claims practices listed in the N.A.I.C. Model Unfair Claims Settlement Practices statute. In addition, twenty-eight unfair practices were discussed, chosen at random from state statutes and state insurance department rules and regulations. It would be no exaggeration to say that another two or three dozen regulations pertaining to claims handling could be added to the practices prohibited by law or regulation that are mentioned in Chapter 4.

Clearly, there is a need to avoid the type of conduct that may result in bad faith litigation and punitive damage awards.

ADJUSTERS' AGGRESSIVE GOOD FAITH
BEHAVIOR

Aggressive good faith behavior is highly essential in today's insurance claims handling environment. By practicing good faith, by making a conscious, honest, diligent effort to act in good faith, the adjuster and the insurer stand an excellent chance to avoid the consequences of bad faith legal actions. The keynote is "aggressive" good faith.

Aggression has a negative connotation. It also has a positive and invaluable connotation for the claims adjuster. To be aggressive contemplates activity that is "vigorously energetic, especially in the use of initiative and forcefulness; boldly assertive and forward." It is "marked by a driving forceful energy or initiative."[3]

As a review of Chapter 4, it is important to point out the aggressive behavior that is required in dealings with the public. Again, try to forget the fact that you are an "insurance claims adjuster." Under today's legal climate and societal expectations, you are a "people adjuster," not a claims adjuster.

As pointed out in Chapter 4, the requirements of the new Unfair Claims Settlement Practices statutes place great emphasis on the following:

1. The "immediate contact rule"
2. Timely and continual communication
3. Diligence
4. Honesty
5. Fairness
6. Reasonableness

The Immediate Contact Rule

The immediate contact rule is probably the most important principle of successful insurance claims handling that can be taught. It is also the embodiment of "aggressive good faith." Immediate contact is absolutely essential to conduct a first-rate investigation. Evidence must be fresh. With delay, the recollections of witnesses dim, and they lose their credibility. Injured parties have time to reflect on the circumstances of an accident and begin to develop resentment and hostility toward persons responsible for their damages. They resent insurance companies that do not give them immediate attention.

In the book, *Human Relations in Handling Insurance Claims*, the author states:

Nobody likes the feeling of being ignored. Our feeling of prestige, of importance, of ego recognition, is damaged if we are avoided by other people whom we believe should be paying us attention. A claimant with a just claim expects attention; he or she is impatient for attention and is insulted if the claim is ignored. If the claimant is not immediately contacted, this damages the claimant's self-respect. He or she feels the need to do something to restore that damaged self-respect. The claimant may feel the need to retaliate—to strike out in anger. Sometimes that anger, plus the real need for legal services, causes the claimant to turn to an attorney for aid.[4]

Timely and Continual Communication

Throughout the preceding chapter dealing with bad faith and unfair claims practices, constant emphasis has been placed upon the failure of the insurer and its employees to do certain things. We note that a number of jurisdictions recognize bad faith actions based upon no more than negligence with regard to claims processing, evaluation, and negotiation. Oftentimes this is nothing more than neglect on the part of the insurance adjuster to communicate with the insured. One court commented that "the fault arose out of bureaucratic bungling and assembly-line inefficiency, not bad faith."[5]

An insurer can be held liable in bad faith actions for its adjusters' heedlessness or carelessness. It is the heighth of heedlessness to fail to communicate. Whether you are morally at fault is irrelevant. An insurer can be held liable for its adjusters' forgetfulness or, even, ignorance.

Remember that you are dealing with the general public on a subject that few people understand. Virtually all of the public is completely ignorant of the principles of tort law relating to negligence. In addition, very few members of the public have the slightest understanding of the principles of insurance. Constant communication with insureds and third-party claimants is necessary in order to explain what is happening in the disposition of the claim. Failure to do so can get your employer into trouble.

The law requires adjusters to make timely and continual communication. The provisions of the N.A.I.C. Model Unfair Claims Settlement Practices statute repeatedly emphasize the need for immediate and continual communication. To avoid a "failure to acknowledge and act reasonably promptly upon communications," you must communicate promptly whenever you receive communications regarding a claim under consideration. "Failing to affirm or deny coverage of claims within a reasonable time" relates directly to a failure of communication. To avoid "failing to provide promptly a reasonable explanation...

for denial of a claim or for the offer of a compromise settlement" requires a prompt and complete communication.

You should again review the fourteen provisions of the N.A.I.C. Model Act and also the variations in the unfair claims statutes that appear in many states' statutes and rules and regulations of the state insurance departments. You will find a constant requirement of communication.

Diligence

Again, an examination of the requirements of the unfair claims settlement statutes and the legal rules regarding good faith conduct places great emphasis upon diligence. *Webster's Collegiate Dictionary* refers to diligence as "persevering application; assiduity (steadily attentive); speed, haste; the attention and care legally expected or required of a person." To be diligent requires a steady, earnest, and energetic application and effort. It requires painstaking effort.

You may look at the stack of pending claims files on your desk, and frustrated by the volume of cases that you are expected to handle, you may wonder how in heaven's name you can be expected to meet the standards of communication and diligence described above. Particularly as claims become more routine, and the stress of work overloads taxes your capacity to meet your case loads, it will be especially hard for you to identify with the legal requirements imposed upon you.

Perhaps the best way to motivate yourself to meet the standard expected of you by the law is to recognize that you may some day be required to testify in court regarding the manner in which you have handled a claim. The ability to avoid personal liability and to keep your employer out of trouble will depend upon your job performance. You must show that you have followed the immediate contact rule, have engaged in timely and continual communication with the insuring public, and have been diligent in going about your business.

Honesty

There is evidence of dishonesty all about us—in government, in business, and in everyday activities. The old adage that "crime does not pay" is frequently mocked by situations where it seems that criminals (particularly white collar criminals) appear to flout the law with impunity without receiving the punishment so richly deserved. This apparent laxness with regard to dishonesty, however, does not serve to excuse or justify it. The Judeo-Christian concept of morality and the standard of morality adopted and enforced by our courts places prime importance on the concept of honesty in the handling of insurance claims, and any hint or suggestion that dishonesty on your part was involved in the handling of a claim can have nothing but dire consequences, both for an adjuster and the adjuster's employer.

Fairness

This entire book has stressed the subject of fairness. Fairness is an organic part of the law of contracts. The whole area of commercial law stresses the concept of fairness. Our business laws were not primarily a product of diligent legislatures. They arose out of the custom and usage of merchants—businessmen who conducted commercial transactions each day. The principles of business law—contract law, agency law, negotiable instruments, security transactions, and all of the other areas of commercial law—were an outgrowth of the conduct of the marketplace.

The basic principles of business law relating to contracts are traceable to the mercantile law ("the Law Merchant") that began to develop during the Renaissance Period. During this period rules of fairness developed in the marketplaces between business individuals to govern their conduct in commercial transactions, particularly in the law of contracts.

An insurance policy is a contract. It is governed by the same rules of fairness which are an intrinsic part of the centuries' old legal principles that govern commercial transactions. Fairness is expected, and constant reference is made to the concept of fairness in the court cases relating to bad faith conduct of insurers and their claims handling personnel.

Reasonableness

An examination of the Unfair Claims Settlement Practices statute shows the importance of reasonable conduct. "Failure to act reasonably," "failing to adopt and implement reasonable standards," failing to conduct "a reasonable investigation," and "failing to affirm or deny coverage of claims within a reasonable time" are all language contained in the N.A.I.C. Model Act. Continuing, "not attempting in good faith to effectuate prompt, fair, and equitable settlements of claims in which liability has become reasonably clear," "failing to promptly settle claims where liability has become reasonably clear under one portion of the insurance policy coverage, in order to influence settlements under other portions of the insurance policy coverage," and "failing to provide promptly a reasonable explanation" or additional references to the word *reasonable* are contained in the Model Act.

We noted in Chapter 2 that bad faith law has evolved to a point where a bad faith judgment may be granted for no more than negligence with regard to claims processing, evaluation, and negotiation. Negligence is exposing others to *unreasonable* risk of harm. Negligence is based upon a legal duty to act in a reasonable manner. Negligence is the failure to conform to that standard of reasonableness, resulting in injury to the interests of another which is caused by the breach of your duty to act reasonably.

Reasonableness is mandatory if one is to practice "aggressive good faith." The failure to act in a reasonable manner is not "aggressive good faith." It may be bad faith conduct. Not all courts today agree that this is the law; however, the trend is unmistakably toward equating unreasonable behavior and bad faith conduct, both in the development of decisional law as well as in the interpretation of the unfair claims settlement practices statutes enacted since 1970.

ADVICE FROM THE EXPERTS

A number of claims experts have written excellent articles dealing with the subject of aggressive good faith and how to avoid bad faith litigation. Major portions of some of these articles reprinted with permission, follow.[6]

"Bad Faith—Bad News"[7]

Clint Miller states that close preventative maintenance on your claims files will minimize your constant exposure to "bad faith" allegations. Although bad faith exposure cannot be eliminated, close attention to each and every claim will minimize the problem. To conduct this close preventative maintenance, it is essential to consider every claim file equally important.

Mr. Miller asks you to visualize yourself as a jury foreman. He asks you whether you would be offended by the conduct of the insurance adjuster in a given case, whether you would be offended by what you saw, you heard, or even the impression you were left with regarding the handling of a given claim. You will be judged on how you have helped the insured, the claimant, or any beneficiaries of the policy.

Any suggestion that you have hindered the people that you are supposed to help violates your responsibility and creates trouble. If you make a mistake, you stand a good chance of exposing your insurer, as well as yourself, to a substantial monetary outlay. The jury will be interested in your service, your attitude, and whether you were perceived as being fair, reasonable, and compassionate with other people's problems.

Checklist for Good Faith Claims Handling The following is Miller's checklist for mitigating exposure to bad faith allegations.

1. Have you thoroughly investigated all facts surrounding the issues presented to you by the insured, the claimant, the agent, or the attorney? The police report in and of itself should not be your investigation. Police reports are not always accurate and are rarely comprehensive. You are required to do your own investigation. Formal reports only aid you in your overall investigation.

2. Have you informed the insured or the claimant of his rights, all his rights, and his obligations under the insurance policy? Did you discuss the arbitration clause, when dealing with the insured, if you and the insured are not able to agree on a settlement of the claim? Don't play games with people. Do not try to be cute or clever.

3. Did you pay the claim in a timely fashion? Unreasonable delay is a prime area of "bad faith litigation." When you do pay the claim and if your payment differs in any way from what the insured thought he had coming, you must accompany the payment with a clarification of any difference. If you pay by "draft," explain what a draft is and also explain that there will be a delay on the claim due to the normal "clearance" procedure after the draft has been deposited in the other party's account.

4. Never make a deceptive representation to any one. If you think or feel a little uncomfortable about anything you are representing to anyone, be honest and tell that person, "I don't know everything." Tell that individual that you will check with your supervisor and get back to him as soon as possible.

5. You cannot request that the insurance policy be canceled in order to deter other policyholders with similar claims from presenting insurance claims against the insurance company. Leave cancellation decisions to the company home office underwriters.

6. You may not manipulate any records, reports, or any other papers to support a denial of coverage. This is dishonesty and fraud.

7. Do not use a claimant's financial situation to devalue the party's bargaining power. In other words, do not take advantage of someone who needs the money badly by offering them much less than they are entitled to recover. These tactics were used thirty years ago, but today, they invite a bad faith lawsuit.

8. You may not make oppressive demands on the insured or the claimant. For example, in a burglary claim, you should not

require the insured to document everything the insured has ever owned. It is common practice in the insurance industry to recognize that not everyone keeps receipts for every item possessed or purchased. You must be reasonable in your demands regarding receipts and documentation. Just remember, the jury foreman probably does not keep many receipts either, and he or she will be judging the reasonableness of your demands on an insured or claimant.

9. You may not unreasonably increase loss reserves on claims when that increase will adversely affect dividends or will increase future premiums of the insured.

10. You may not tell the insured or the claimant not to talk to an attorney, or not to retain legal counsel. At least one state, California, specifically prohibits you from advising the other party, even a third-party claimant, not to obtain an attorney. It is likely that similar conduct in some other states will be construed as unfair and unreasonable conduct and subject you to bad faith liability.

11. You must answer letters of inquiry and return phone calls by insureds, claimants, and attorneys. This is not only a basic, common professional courtesy, but you are also required by statute in some states to answer these letters of inquiry and return telephone calls in a timely manner. Some statutes specify the number of days that you have by law to communicate or take certain action. As a practical matter, when you return a phone call, you should provide complete documentation as to the month, day, year, and the time of day the call was returned, and what the essence of the conversation was with the party with whom you spoke. This documentation is absolutely essential, since it may be subpoenaed in a court action.

Documentation can serve as excellent evidence to show that you have handled a case with dispatch, providing timely and continual communication. The absence of such information can strongly prejudice your case. When someone reviews your file, the file should be like an open book showing a history and the development of the claim. This history should continue until the claim has been paid or denied.

Always remember that your claim file is subject to subpoena and may be examined by a court and jury. Your file must be exemplary and complete. If you have a detailed, complete log of all of the communications that you have had with the insured or third-party claimant, you convey the impression of professionalism and fairness in a court of law.

On the other hand, an attempt in court to verify the fact that you have made some phone calls or have had conversations that were not logged in your file is very difficult. You will find it difficult to recall dates and times of making the calls, even if they do exist, and at best, you will appear as an incompetent person before the jury. At the worst, you may be perceived as a liar.

12. You must affirm or deny coverage issues in a timely fashion and with specificity.

13. Once coverage for liability becomes reasonably clear, you are then required to communicate your decision, with supporting evidence in the event of a denial, or pay the claim promptly.

14. If you are going to deny a claim, get a second opinion. Many companies make this a mandatory requirement. Particularly if you are unsure of coverage questions, it is highly necessary for you to discuss the matter with underwriting personnel and probably your legal counsel. It is simply amazing how some losses that you have always considered to be not covered under your insurance policy have suddenly been interpreted by the courts to be insured.

15. If the insured or claimant has two or more separate elements of the overall claim, you may not "hold out" on the payment of one portion of the overall claim to coerce settlement of the other claim. You must pay each and every element of the claim as it becomes reasonably clear that payment is due and owing, without withholding payment on one portion pending settlement on another portion.

16. You may not compel the insured or claimant to institute litigation in order to recover any or all of their benefits under the insurance policy if coverage is reasonably clear. At the least, your insurer can be held responsible for reasonable attorney fees should the insured or claimant unnecessarily have to institute litigation to recover benefits under the policy of insurance. At the worst, you may subject yourself and your employer to a bad faith action with resultant punitive damages.

17. You must always be uniform in payment of similar claims. Discrimination among claimants and/or insureds is probably "bad faith per se," or "strict liability bad faith."

18. If you are requested by the insured to tell what payments have been made to a third party under a policy of insurance, you must comply with this request and document any and all payments made under the policy.

19. You are never to inform a claimant or an insured to go ahead and get an attorney, and if they win in court, you will only take

it up on appeal, and tie them up in the legal system for a long time. You cannot tell them "you must settle with me" (the adjuster) for whatever "I feel the case is worth." You must negotiate. You must generate a dialogue between yourself and the party with whom you are attempting to settle a claim, whether that be the insured, the claimant, or an attorney.

20. If you secure a settlement from the insured covering essentially the same information as on a Proof of Loss form, then a formal Proof of Loss form may be redundant. Requiring a redundant Proof of Loss could be interpreted to be "harassment," which would lead to an allegation of "bad faith" claims practices.

21. Give a written explanation as to any denial of a claim or compromise of a claim based on the coverage language in the policy.

22. Never mislead anyone as to the applicable Statute of Limitations for a bodily injury claim or a property damage claim, and so on. If you are not sure about the Statute of Limitations as it applies to the insurance policy or any oral contract made, or regarding the time limit on making a personal injury claim, you should consult with your supervisor. Get the answer in writing.

Degrees of Bad Faith Some jurisdictions, such as California, recognize two degrees of bad faith. The first type of bad faith could be called *deliberate bad faith.* Deliberate bad faith is bad faith in which one knowingly is guilty of misconduct. It involves malice, oppression, and/or fraud. It shows a "conscious disregard of a party's rights." It is the type of bad faith action where juries have been most receptive to awarding punitive damages to punish the misconduct of the individual as well as to discourage others from engaging in the same type of misconduct.

The second type of bad faith is what might be termed *innocent bad faith.* This would be the type of bad faith which arises from the developing trend of courts to award bad faith damages in cases of simple negligence. As Magarick states: "Some courts continue to confuse the doctrines of bad faith and negligence as basic requirements for liability in excess of the policy limits."[8]

In cases involving innocent bad faith, the defendant must be able to demonstrate to the jury and/or the judge that there was an absence of malice, oppression, fraud, or a "conscious disregard" of the other party's rights. It is here that your claims file can do much to illustrate your honesty, fairness, and reasonableness. You must maintain a professional demeanor, avoiding conduct that can be interpreted to be capricious or arbitrary. Engaging in personally repugnant behavior, showing ill will toward the insured or third-party claimant, invites trouble.

A professional claims file, in which you have handled communication matters with diligence, honesty, fairness, and reasonableness can do much to help you avoid the deliberate bad faith action. However, being human, it is inevitable that sooner or later you will make a mistake—an honest mistake—that may subject your employer to a bad faith action. If this occurs, you should do as much as possible to mitigate or minimize the potential damages. Probably your smartest approach, according to Clint Miller, is to apologize, in writing if necesssary. An adjuster will not look as bad to a jury if the adjuster has admitted a human error—an honest mistake. Possibly this could sway the jury and mitigate entirely any allegation of conscious disregard of the other party's rights.

"Bad Faith—Bad News II"[9]

In another article, Mr. Miller contends that bad faith litigation is usually the result of a problem arising in one of the following areas: training; listening; documenting; expediting; and educating.

Training Poor training of adjusters or inexperience can lead to bad faith actions. This is particularly true in complex, problem cases. In the first place, the insured may not receive the service to which he or she is entitled by contract, and that in and of itself could be the beginning of a bad faith situation. Further, poorly trained adjusters can create many mistakes, including misrepresentation of facts as well as failing to follow company procedures, conduct proper investigations, or do other things which are expected of competent claims adjusters. Miller states that many companies have been reluctant to extensively train adjusters because they may leave, after training, to join a competitor.

Listening Claims adjusters, perhaps more than most other people, must be good listeners. The adjuster's first contact with the public may be in a time of crisis. Insureds expect the type of service that they have paid for and they expect someone to listen to their problems.

Continual emphasis has been placed in this book on the subject of communication. Communication is not just speaking. It is a two-way street. Communication involves speaking *and listening* by both parties.

No claims adjuster can do a decent job handling an insurance claim without listening carefully. Careful listening is an important part of a proper claims investigtion, securing all of the pertinent facts that are necessary to establish a good evidential claims file.

Elaborating on listening, a number of people have written about the "inside adjuster" versus the "outside adjuster." Some claims experts contend that telephone adjusting is an inadequate way to handle complex and serious claims. Others suggest that the economies of telephone adjusting more than compensate for the lack of personal contact. Nevertheless, there is a valid point regarding whether communication is accomplished better by telephone contact or by personal contact.

Telephone adjusting is more demanding, in a sense, than personal contact. It is harder to communicate by telephone. That is why extra attention must be devoted to communication by telephone.

Documenting Mr. Miller points out that a good faith file contains a chronological summary of each and every event that has taken place concerning that claim. Complete documentation of files serves two useful purposes. One, it enables the adjuster to perform the adjusting task more thoroughly and effectively; and, two, it is proof to an outside observer (or jury) that the claim was handled in good faith.

Expediting The number one cause of bad faith litigation is the unreasonable delay in the paying or processing of an insurance claim. When an adjuster quits or is fired, his or her files should be reassigned immediately in order to provide for continuity in the claims handling. Otherwise, the insurer is in danger of bad faith litigation situations. Files cannot just sit around.

Another point Miller makes is that adjusters cannot be overloaded. An overworked, overloaded adjuster finds it difficult to expedite claims files. Overloads should be assigned to an independent adjustment company. This is a major reason why independents came into being.

No more than twenty-four hours should elapse from the time a claim is received by the claims department until the insured or claimant is contacted. When the insured or claimant is contacted, it should be standard operating procedure to provide the adjuster's first and last name; the name, address, and phone number of the company the adjuster represents; and the claim or file number assigned to the claim. This information assures that an insured or claimant is not abandoned.

Educating Perhaps this section should be entitled, "Education of Insureds and Claimants." Adjusters must educate insureds and claimants. The party must be informed what is expected in order to handle the claim. For example, the insured must be advised of the policy requirements regarding notice and substantiation of damages. It is also necessary to educate the insured regarding matters involving potential excess liability.

If an insured and insurer cannot agree on specific matters, such as the amount of damages, there are procedures that determine what should be submitted to arbitration. The insurance industry has a formal arbitration board available to help in case of a stalemate. The board's decision can be binding or non-binding depending on the wishes of the insurer or insured. It is important to make insureds and claimants aware of the opportunity to have a disinterested third party review the claim. When an insured or claimant is informed of this option, it presents a reasonable next step in the process. Failure to suggest this option leaves no alternative but the courts. The courthouse is not the only place to settle honest differences of opinion.

The third-party claimant has traditionally occupied the position of an adversary who has no contractual relationship to the parties of the liability policy. Nevertheless, the advent of extra-contractual liability imposed by law in a number of jurisdictions, giving third parties a direct cause of action against the insurance company, suggests that insurance adjusters must treat claimants the same as they do insureds. This necessitates advising the claimant of their legal options, including the right to obtain an attorney, if they so desire. It also involves the necessity to inform the claimant and to try and educate him or her concerning the law of damages. The law of damages requires that claimants substantiate the amount of their damages.

"Living with Bad Faith"[10]

Henry Miller provides guidance on how to avoid bad faith actions. His advice takes the form of "The Ten Commandments of Bad Faith."

Foolishly Economizing The First Commandment: Thou shalt not be a hero. This advice relates to the futile attempt on the part of a claims adjuster or claims counsel to attempt to economize on a case where the gravity of the injuries and damages of the claimant are so severe in relation to policy limits that it is an obviously futile exercise to attempt to "save" part of those policy limits. It also applies where a company has given authorization for settlement up to a certain amount, and the adjuster or defense counsel unwisely attempts to save a few dollars from the amount authorized when the authorized amount appears to be an appropriate settlement.

It is a particularly dangerous practice to attempt to save the company a few dollars when the company has advised the adjuster or insurance counsel to pay the amount stipulated. Counsel for the defense who disobeys the instruction does so at his own peril. In one 1977 Illinois case, for example, the appellate court held that an insurance company could bring a malpractice action against the defense attorney who had failed to communicate authorization for a settlement which ultimately resulted in the insurance company's exposure for excess liability over the policy limits.[11]

Ignoring Advice of Defense Counsel The Second Commandment: Thou shalt listen, under pain of excess liability, to the advice of defense counsel. Henry Miller warns that claims personnel can get into trouble by ignoring the advice of defense counsel.

The danger is particularly severe, since the claims files on bad faith matters are subject to discovery by the plaintiff's attorney. Thus, if the claims file is replete with letters saying, "This is a bad one"; "You better look out"; "Pay this"; and "This one could go over the policy," an insurer's failure to heed such warnings could result in a powerful claim of bad faith.

Whether you are dealing with outside defense counsel or with staff attorneys, the advice of defense counsel should not be ignored. Remember also, inter-office memoranda discussing liability and exposure have been admitted as evidence in bad faith lawsuits.[12]

Keep Your Insured Advised The Third Commandment: Thou shalt keep the insured advised. Relating to the Second Commandment, if claims personnel have received advice of defense counsel regarding the possible outcome of a case or the amount of liability involved, there is an absolute obligation to inform the insured. Courts have spelled out this duty:

> A duty is imposed on the company to communicate to the insured the results of any investigation indicating liability in excess of the policy limits and any offers of settlements which have been made, so that he may take proper steps to protect his own interest.[13]

The "ad damnum" excess letter, sent by the insurance company, advises the insured that there is a good possibility that the claim of the plaintiff and a subsequent judgment may exceed the policy limits. The letter advises insureds that they have the right to secure independent counsel at their own expense to represent them for any such excess liability.

The "ad damnum" letter is rather routinely used by many companies, particularly where it appears there is any possibility whatsoever that the amount in controversy may exceed the policy limits. It is probably prudent conduct on the part of an insurer to send out such a letter routinely in cases of serious personal injuries where insureds have only standard liability limits under their policies.

It is also safe to say that the insurer is obligated to respond accurately to requests from its insured with reference to the progress of any settlement negotiation. This point was particularly spelled out in a 1976 New York case where an insured, while being interviewed by a representative of the insurer, inquired as to demands and offers. The claims representative declined to disclose this information on the grounds that it was "against company policy." An excess judgment was awarded the plaintiffs, and the insurer argued that the tender of the full policy limits on the eve of trial automatically insulated it from any liability for bad faith failure to settle within the policy limits. The court rejected this viewpoint and further stated: "We are of the view...that the carrier is obliged in most circumstances to respond accurately to requests from its insured with reference to the progress of any settlement negotiations." The court further ruled that the insurance adjuster's refusal, on the grounds of company policy, in response to the insured's direct inquiry to disclose "how much was being asked and how much was being offered" was relevant on the issue of bad faith.[14]

Handling Multiple Claims under the Same Policy The Fourth Commandment: Thou shalt not deplete the policy carelessly when there are multiple claims. Henry Miller points out that an insurer that wishes to pay policy limits but is confronted with multiple claims is in a delemma. If it settles some claims but others go to judgment which cannot be satisfied by an exhausted policy, the company may be liable for bad faith.

The practical solution would be to call for a conference, offer the policy to all the claimants and hope that with the aid of the court, a distribution is agreed upon. If unable to resolve the problem with a conference, the prudent insurer might attempt to file an "interpleader" action. This suit pulls all the claimants together into court where they must agree how the policy limits are to be divided.

When an insurer is confronted with multiple claims and is concerned that the policy limits will be inadequate to cover all of the claims, the law usually allows interpleader. When several claimants claim the same fund (that is, the limits of the policy), and the insurer is uncertain which of the claimants has a right to the fund, the insurer runs the risk that, if some claimants are paid and others are not, it may subsequently incur bad faith liability. Thus, the insurer may file an "interpleader" suit, which requires the claimants to litigate their right to the fund in question. Remember, however, in matters involving insureds, there is always the duty to defend an insured, and an insurer cannot dismiss itself from the claims situation by use of the interpleader device.

Proper Investigation The Fifth Commandment: Thou shalt investigate properly. We have discussed this point in considerable detail in the chapter regarding bad faith conduct of insurers. Since bad faith law may evolve toward imposing liability upon insurers for ordinary negligence, it is clear that the failure to do a good job in investigating the insured's liability obviously exposes an insurer to liability.

The cause of action may arise out of mere negligence or out of a simple case of breach of contract—the breach of the implied covenant of good faith that the insurer will act in a manner that does not impair the legal rights of the insured. It was clearly spelled out in the 1957 landmark decision of *Brown v. Guarantee Insurance Company* that the insurer is in trouble if there is an inadequate investigation conducted of the insured's liability.[15]

Try to Settle The Sixth Commandment: Thou shalt explore the possibility of settlement. At one time an insurer could sit back, relax, and have no duty to initiate settlement discussion. Prior to modern discovery rules, the plaintiff's attorney usually did not know the policy limits, and it was a cardinal rule that insurers did not volunteer this information in most cases. Consequently, plaintiff's counsel usually had insufficient information upon which to base a settlement demand. As Henry Miller states: "When there was no demand within the policy, there was a sense of euphoria back at the company."

A 1974 New Jersey case changed this line of reasoning. In the Rova Farms Resort case, the court ruled that the "insurer has an affirmative duty to explore settlement possibilities."[16] A Wisconsin court agreed, ruling that the "insurer should initiate settlement discussion in a limited policy case.[17]

Think Bad Faith The Seventh Commandment: Thou shalt think bad faith. The possibility of a bad faith action must be considered in all cases. However, it is particularly important in cases where there is a policy with inadequate limits.

In every step of the claims investigation and settlement negotiations, the claims representative and insurance counsel must maintain the highest level of professional conduct, communicating constantly with the insured, making certain that the investigation is a model of completeness and demonstrated diligence, and that all settlement negotiations are conducted with diligence and intelligence.

Of particular importance is the need for the adjuster and insurance counsel to respond immediately and with diligence to communications by the plaintiff's attorney. If settlement offers are made within the policy limits, the insurer must be diligent in evaluating the demands. Such diligence requires that the insurer and its claims representatives make a thorough, intelligent, and informed evaluation of a plaintiff's damages.

Even then, however, the claims adjuster must think bad faith. There are other factors to consider besides the matter of damages. The adjuster may have made a well-informed evaluation of the plaintiff's damages. However, one must also evaluate what may happen if the case goes to trial. You must consider thoroughly the question of liability. Even the best legal experts on the law can conclude that a case is a no-liability situation. However, once the case goes before a jury, juries begin to think of other factors besides liability. They are concerned about the magnitude of the plaintiff's injuries, and they will sympathize with the plaintiff. If the insured is a large corporation, many juries will be prejudiced against such a defendant.

Further, there must be an intelligent evaluation of witnesses and the impression that such witnesses may make upon the jury. One psychological phenomenon that is well documented is called the "Liking-Leniency Hypothesis." In essence, it means that how well we like an individual bears a significant relationship to how well we treat that individual. The concept is explained in the book, *Human Relations in Handling Insurance Claims:*

> From a legal standpoint, how attractive a plaintiff or defendant is to the jury should be irrelevant to court judgments. Unfortunately, this probably is not the case. Researchers contend that there is strong evidence that jurors favor a plaintiff or defendant who is likable or attractive, or who possesses attitudes similar to those of the jurors. This is the liking-leniency hypothesis. A number of studies purport to document preferential treatment to the party considered to be attractive to the jury. In criminal cases, for example, a male jury tends to judge an attractive woman defendant to be less guilty, recommending more lenient prescriptions for punishment than in the case of the not-so-attractive defendant.[18]

Resolve Cases in a Timely Manner The Eighth Commandment: Thou shalt consider plaintiff's demands and not take all eternity. Waiting for settlements of cases until "reaching the courthouse steps" is no longer advisable. A number of court decisions have expressed impatience at such dilatory tactics, ruling that an insurer violates its fiduciary responsibility in not attempting to resolve the case in a more timely manner.

Furthermore, the Unfair Claims Settlement Practices Statute which most states have in existence today provides that: "Not attempting in good faith to effectuate prompt, fair and equitable settlements of claims in which liability has become reasonably clear" is prohibited. Of course, this provision relates to cases in which liability has become reasonably clear. If we are dealing in cases of disputed liability, one might argue that delay and dilatory tactics are a valid, legitimate defense tactic. However, courts have ruled that belated offers *after rejection of an early settlement offer* can subject an insurer to bad faith liability.

This duty of timeliness certainly is valid in cases involving clear-cut liability. In those cases, however, where claims adjusters and insurance counsel have concluded that there is doubtful or disputed liability, it seems to be an unfair requirement to deny the insurer the right to use defensive tactics of delay and procrastination. The insurer, however, can avoid the appearance of delay and procrastination if it maintains a continuing dialogue with both the plaintiff's attorney and the insured, constantly attempting to settle the claim commensurate with the liability exposure perceived by insurance counsel. The duty, essentially, is one of communication. It does not mandate that claims must be paid merely because they are presented.

Inducing Insured to Contribute   The Ninth Commandment: Thou shalt not induce the insured to contribute. Years ago some insurance companies would seek a contribution from the insured before the insurer would deplete its policy. This is clearly not tolerated today, and courts have ruled that exhorting the insured to contribute something "was in itself suggestive of bad faith."

Your Duty to Insured—Good Faith   The Tenth Commandment: Thou shalt consider the insured's interest. This, of course, is the greatest of the commandments since it embraces all of the others. "The law imposes upon the insurer the obligation of good faith—basically the duty to consider, in good faith, the insured's interests as well as its own when making decisions as to settlement."[19]

"Excess Liability for Bad Faith, or Is There More to It?"[20]

John H. Holmes has drawn up a simple checklist of behavior that is essential in order to avoid bad faith liability. You will note that most of the following suggestions have already been discussed.

Mr. Holmes states that claims need:

1. Prompt attention.
2. Adequate investigation—prompt evaluation of facts.
3. Proper analysis of coverage (factually and legally).
4. Proper evaluation of liability exposure (factually and legally).
5. Proper evaluation of potential area of damage award (factually and legally).
6. Communication with insured:
   a. regarding facts;
   b. regarding damage claims;
   c. regarding getting independent counsel;
   d. regarding settlement offers and demands (and regarding insured's option to contribute to settlement);
   e. regarding investigation and evaluation;
   f. regarding any and all coverage limitations.

7. Compliance with the Unfair Claims Practices Act and/or other statutes or administrative rules and regulations.
8. Treating the interests of the insured with the same consideration as the interests of the insurer: all handling and all decisions regarding handling and/or settlement must be done based upon the hypothetical assumption that the insurer would be liable and responsible for the entire amount.

Mr. Holmes also points out some additional factors that are most important in avoiding bad faith exposure. For example, he stresses the importance of targeting the problem files. We have already suggested that all files should be given equal weight and equal attention. However, it is only natural that some files will suggest problems which must receive constant and intensive attention. These are the problem files.

Another point brought out in his article is the need for the use of experienced personnel. A claims manager should not use the excuse of burdensome case loads to assign serious problem files to inexperienced personnel.

Another point brought out by Mr. Holmes is "don't oversimplify or develop mindsets." A mindset has been described as a tendency on the part of people to develop an inflexible state of mind where everything seems to fit in a particular position or posture so that one always assumes that if a set of conditions is present that a given result will occur. A mindset suggests an inflexibility of thinking and a tendency to discard the possibility that some inconsistent consequence may result from a given action. It rejects the unexpected.

Mr. Holmes illustrates some situations where inflexibility and rigidity of thinking—mindsets—result in unexpected consequences. He states that there is a continuing inclination in attitude of insurers, adjusters, and defense attorneys, to over-simplify excess exposure.

Illustrative reactions of insurance industry personnel to unexpected consequences include:

That can't be bad faith. We didn't think it was a liability situation.

That can't be bad faith. We relied on our defense attorney.

That can't be bad faith. The plaintiff's attorney didn't give us enough time to respond to the demand.

That can't be bad faith. The facts are disputed and we have the right to believe our insured.

That can't be bad faith. We didn't know about the plaintiff's surprise witness.

That can't be bad faith. We didn't know our witness would change his story or make a bad impression.

"Claims People Beware—Be Careful Out There"[21]

Robert J. Brown presents an interesting narrative of a situation in which he was called upon as consultant. He was asked to scrutinize the claims files of an insurer in order to determine the timeliness of claims procedures, investigations, evaluations, negotiations, and the major documentary needs in the handling of insurance claims. He subsequently served as an expert witness on some sixty claims situations in which the plaintiffs alleged mishandling of specific files that he had previously examined. He concludes that, with only a few isolated exceptions, most insurers do a fair job. Firms that fail to meet good claims handling standards fail for a number of reasons, including the following:

1. *Poor Reserving Practices.* Some insurers fail to properly utilize and complete a reserve computation form to detail how and on what basis the figures were reached.
2. *Improper Benefits Paid.* On workers compensation cases improper benefits are paid usually when the employer fails to note that an employee is only a part-timer or is a seasonal worker.
3. *Delays in Accident Reporting and Claim Files Set-up.* Usually the set-up is late due to the late filing of the first report, but at times the report is late and the file material lays around for a few days in the claims office before it is finally set up.
4. *Delays in the Assignment of Claims to a Supervisor or Adjuster.* This is usually a procedural problem that can be remedied by a change in procedure.
5. *Delays in Completing the Investigations.* This practice can usually be blamed on weak or inadequate supervision. A poor diary system or other procedural problems may also be contributing factors.
6. *Minimal or No Involvement on the Part of Claims Personnel.* The failure to involve the actual claims personnel in the evaluation and negotiations of claims is a serious error on the part of insurers. It seems imprudent to leave out the people who are the most familiar with the claim when it comes to evaluating and negotiating claims.
7. *Delays in Closing Inactive and/or Settled Claims.* This arises from a breakdown in the claims flow and results in a backlog of reserves on claims on which the reserves should be removed.
8. *Little or No Coordination of Activities or Interaction Between People.* It is a serious error to have virtually no communication or interaction between the insured/client, claimant, physicians, attorneys, and claims people. This usually is

corrected with a little education about the role of the claims person as a participant in a coordinator of all claims activities pertaining to the claims assigned.

One point that is particularly emphasized by Mr. Brown is the subject of documentation. The phrase used repeatedly during claims reviews is: "Remember, if it ain't there, it don't count." A file that is not documented has little evidential value. Everything should be written down in a professional and timely manner. Then when the file is reviewed, the notes and other documentation will be read, and proper credit and other consideration can be given to the file. You are advised to write down notes regarding the aspect of the claim involved and, as explained earlier in this book, put the exact time and date of the communication and sign your name. Writing should include a detail of your thinking and reasoning for decisions made and action taken. Again, make certain that you avoid any personal prejudices or conduct that may suggest that you are acting in an arbitrary or capricious manner.

"Avoiding Judgments for Punitive Damages"[22]

John D. Ingram and Ralph J. Elwart make an important observation:

> Although insurers will insist that they are aware of the situation, and no doubt they are at the management level, *it is open to serious question whether the claims personnel at the customer contact level are aware of the ramifications of their actions.* (Emphasis added.)

The primary point of this book is to make you aware of the ramifications of your actions and to keep you and your insurer-employer out of trouble.

Elwart and Ingram are particularly concerned with the quality of communication with insureds, pointing out that telephone conversations and correspondence are frequently the only contacts with an insured. Unless these are handled properly, the stage is set for trouble.

The authors declare: "In no other industry is the standard for operating in good faith so high," and they go on to review the requirements imposed by the unfair claims settlement practices statutes. They then list some of the steps which should be considered by adjusters in the progress of a claim:

1. Acknowledge receipt of correspondence in a timely manner.
2. Obtain all investigative information initially, as opposed to one report at a time.

3. Document all transactions that occur on a particular file, whether it be a telephone call, a letter from the insured or a file review.
4. Keep the insured informed of the progress of the claim on a periodic basis.
5. If the insured will be receiving less than expected in settlement of the claim, thoroughly explain the pertinent reasons.
6. If the claim is to be denied, provide *all* of the reasons, and include a "reservations of rights" paragraph in the letter to the insured (a paragraph which preserves any defenses which the insurer may not be aware of at the time of the denial).
7. Be aware of the peculiarities of the laws of the various states, and how that impacts on the claim at hand.
8. When reviewing a denial of benefits, evaluate the claim file as a potential suit, which it surely is.
9. When negotiating a claim, a certain amount of "puffing" is expected, but *do not* misrepresent the facts of the claim or the coverage involved.

The foregoing list, of course, duplicates much of the advice given throughout this book, but it does not hurt to read the same advice twice—and have its validity reinforced by a number of authorities.

Elwart and Ingram advise that judgments for punitive damages can be avoided at the claims handling stage, after the litigation has been initiated, and on appeal. Immediately before and during litigation, there are opportunities to avoid punitive damages. The authors describe three situations that are directly addressed by the Unfair Claims Settlement Practices statutes:

1. Subsection (f) requires a good faith effort to settle when liability becomes reasonably clear. The authors point out that it is quite possible that, in some cases, liability will be somewhat doubtful in the early stages, but will later become "reasonably clear," and at this point, the duty to make a good faith settlement effort will arise.
2. Subsection (g) prohibits "compelling claimants to institute litigation to recover amounts due...by offering substantially less than the amounts ultimately recovered...by analogy, this guideline would certainly indicate that it is bad faith for an insurer to force claimants to continue litigation or take an appeal because of the insurer's refusal to pay a valid claim.
3. Subsection (k) suggests that it is bad faith to threaten litigation to avoid an unfavorable arbitration award. By analogy, this could be readily applied to an insurer's forcing the claimant to

file suit or respond to an appeal in order to collect a claim clearly due and owing.

In conclusion, the authors declare that at every point from first notice of claim to final affirmance on appeal, there are pitfalls and traps where the unwary, inexperienced, and careless claims person may incur liability for punitive damages. Yet for the prudent and informed, each of these same points presents an opportunity to avoid such liability and, in the process, to earn the confidence and good will of the insuring public.

SUPERVISOR'S RESPONSIBILITY

Former President Harry Truman had a sign on his desk which read "The buck stops here." President Truman's view in stating that a superior has the responsibility for the actions of his or her subordinates was entirely accurate. In claims handling, this responsibility entails not only the training and education of new claims adjusters but also the close, day-by-day supervision of adjusters' activities.

Claims adjusters come in all shapes, forms, and dispositions. Some new claims adjusters will develop into outstanding practitioners. Others are unsuited by temperament, disposition, or work habits to be in the field. The supervisor must quickly ascertain whether an individual is suited for this occupation. Failure by the superior to keep close tabs on new claims representatives can easily result in bad faith situations developing because of the conduct of the claims adjuster. Some conduct can result from ignorance of company adjusting procedure and contract and tort law, and other kinds of conduct can result from laziness and personality defects of new personnel.

Particularly important for new claims personnel is to recognize the supervisory responsibility of their superiors. Adjusters who do not know the answer to questions must be trained to ask. Adjusters are not expected to be ultimate authorities on claims adjusting and the law of contracts and torts from their first days on the job. Supervisors should answer questions and decide what procedures adjusters should follow in specific situations.

Chapter Notes

1. John H. Holmes, "Excess Liability for Bad Faith, or Is There More To It?" *The Independent Adjuster* (Summer 1984), pp. 8-9.

2. John D. Long, "A Review of the Doctrine of Punitive Damages," *Liability Beyond the Insurance Contract,* The Society of Chartered Property and Casualty Underwriters, Winter 1985, pp. 1-11.

3. *The Random House Dictionary of the English Language* (New York: Random House, 1966) and *Webster's Seventh New Collegiate Dictionary* (Springfield, MA: G&C Merriam Co., 1970).

4. Willis Park Rokes, *Human Relations in Handling Insurance Claims,* Revised Edition (Homewood, IL: Richard D. Irwin, Inc., 1981), pp. 349-350.

5. *Robertson v. Hartford,* 333 F. Supp. 739 (D. C. Ore. 1970).

6. Where appropriate, the author has clarified or expanded on the experts' materials and takes responsibility for any misinterpretations.

7. Clint Miller, "Bad Faith—Bad News," *CAIIA Newsletter* (California Association of Independent Insurance Adjusters, January 1986), pp. 1, 6-7.

8. Pat Magarick, *Excess Liability,* 2nd ed. (New York: Clark Boardman Co., Ltd., 1982), p. 204.

9. Clint Miller, "Bad Faith—Bad News II," *CAIIA Newsletter* (California Association of Independent Insurance Adjusters, September 1986), pp. 1, 7.

10. Henry G. Miller, "Living with Bad Faith," *Insurance Counsel Journal* (January 1979), pp. 34-43.

11. *Smiley v. Manchester Insurance and Indemnity Co.,* 49 Ill. App. 3rd 675, 364 N.E.2d 683 (1977).

12. *Henke v. Iowa Mutual Insurance Co.,* 97 N.W.2d 168 (Iowa, 1959).

13. *Bollinger v. Nuss,* 202 Kan. 326 at 339 (Kansas 1969).

14. *Knobloch v. Royal Globe Insurance Company,* 381 N.Y.S. 2nd 433, 38 N.Y. 2nd 471, 344 N.E. 2nd 364 (N.Y., 1976).

15. *Brown v. Guarantee Insurance Company,* 319 P. 2d 69 (Cal. 1957).

16. *Rova Farms Resort, Inc. v. Investors Insurance Company of America,* 323 Atl. 2d 495 (N.J. 1974).

17. *Alt v. American Family Mutual Insurance Co.,* 71 Wis. 2d 340, 237 N.W.2d 706 (Wis. 1976).

18. Rokes, p. 326.

19. *Cappano v. Phoenix Assurance of New York,* 28 App. Div. 2d 639 (N.Y., 1967).

20. Holmes, pp. 8-9.

21. Robert J. Brown, "Claims People Beware—Be Careful Out There," *CAIIA Newsletter* (California Association of Independent Insurance Adjusters, October 1985), pp. 1, 6.

22. John D. Ingram and Ralph J. Elwart, Jr., "Avoiding Judgments for Punitive Damages," *Insurance Counsel Journal* (January 1980), pp. 45-52.

Bibliography

"The Bad-Faith Bears." *Insurance Adjuster*, December 1982.

Brown, Robert J. "Claims People Beware—Be Careful Out There." *CAIIA Newsletter*, October 1985.

Donaldson, James H. *Casualty Claim Practice*, 4th ed. Homewood, IL: Richard D. Irwin, 1984.

Good Faith. Schaumburg, IL: Insurance Committee for Arson Control, January 1986.

Hair, Mattox S. and Nicolas V. Pugliano, Jr. "Discovery of the Insurance Investigator's Claim File." *For the Defense*, January 1986.

Hatch, Michael A. " 'Unfair Claims Practices Act' Creates Positive Cause of Action." *Minnesota Trial Lawyer*, Special Edition, 1984.

Holmes, John H. "Excess Liability for Bad Faith, or Is There More to It?" *The Independent Adjuster*, Summer 1984.

Insurance Litigation Reporter. June 1986, pp. 1033-1036.

Leo, Jeffrey H. *Perspectives*. Los Angeles: Parkenson, Wolf, Lazar, and Leo, June 1986.

Levit, Victor B. "Recent Developments in Bad Faith and Punitive Damages." *CPCU Journal*, March 1985.

Long, John D. "A Review of the Doctrine of Punitive Damages." *Liability Beyond the Insurance Contract*, Malvern, PA: Society of CPCU, Winter 1985.

Magarick, Pat. *Excess Liability*, 2nd ed. New York: Clark Boardman Co., Ltd., 1982.

Martin, Frederic H. "Claims Investigation: A Cost-Cutting Casualty?" *Risk Management*, June 1986.

Miller, Clint. "Bad Faith—Bad News," *CAIIA Newsletter*, January 1986.

————. "Bad Faith—Bad News II." *CAIIA Newsletter*, September 1986.

Miller, Henry G. "Living with Bad Faith." *Insurance Counsel Journal*, January 1979.

Mehr, Robert I. and Emerson Cammack. *Principles of Insurance*. Homewood, IL: Richard D. Irwin, 1976.

Prosser, William L. *Handbook of the Law of Torts*, 4th ed. St. Paul: West Publishing Company, 1971.

"Punitive Damages." *FC&S Bulletins*—Casualty and Surety, April 1984.

134—Bibliography

Rokes, Willis Park. *Human Relations in Handling Insurance Claims.*
Homewood, IL: Richard D. Irwin, 1981.

_____."Legislative Intent Under the State Unfair Claims Settlement Practices Statute—Are Private Rights of Action Foreclosed?" *The Journal of Insurance Regulation,* June 1984.

Steiner, George A. and John F. Steiner. *Business, Government and Society,* 4th ed. New York: Random House Business Division, 1985.

Index

A

Actual damages, influence of, on punitive damages awards, *70*

Adequacy or excessiveness of punitive damages, *63*

Adjusters, bad faith actions against, *38*

"inside," *10*

"outside," *9*

Adjusters' aggressive good faith behavior, *109*

Administrative remedy, exclusivity of, *82*

"Affected with a public interest," *80*

Aggression, displaced, *3*

Aggressive good faith, *107*

cardinal requirements of, *93*

Aggressive good faith behavior, adjusters', *109*

American Law Reports, *64*

Anti-social viewpoint, *7*

Arbitrary, capricious, indifferent, or irresponsible conduct, *36*

Arguments advanced by insurers against insuring punitive damages, *73*

Arson and burglary claims, *41*

Attorney-client privilege, *15*

Attorney's advice, rejection of, *30*

Attorneys, increase in, *17*

"Avoiding Judgments for Punitive Damages," *128*

B

Bad faith, *14, 25*

additional factors contributing to, *31*

comparative, *39*

degrees of, *117*

deliberate, *117*

early history of, *27*

factors contributing to, *28*

innocent, *117*

as a mere breach of contract, *50*

and negligence, *44*

and punitive damages, *50*

rationale and definition of, *25*

Ten Commandments of, *120*

as a tort, *50*

Bad faith actions against adjusters, *38*

"Bad Faith—Bad News," *113*

"Bad Faith—Bad News II," *118*

Bad faith cases, common, *40*

Bad faith law, modern, *28*

Brassil v. Maryland Casualty Co., *27*

Breach of contract, bad faith as, *50*

Brown, Robert J., *127*

Brown v. Guarantee Insurance Company, *28*

135

Y